P9-CDK-617

WILLIAMS-SONOMA

THE ART OF PRESERVING

AUTHORS

Lisa Atwood, Rebecca Courchesne, Rick Field

PHOTOGRAPHER

France Ruffenach

weldon**owen**

Contents

SALSAS, RELISHES & CHUTNEYS

CONDIMENTS & SAUCES

REFERENCE

Almost everyone has a memory about preserving.

Maybe your family put up dill pickles every summer, using cucumbers harvested from the backyard garden. Or you remember picking plump berries in the hot afternoon sun, then helping your mother turn them, magically, into jams and jellies for the breakfast table. Or you recall the first time you bit into a scone slathered with blood orange marmalade.

When faced with an abundance of local produce, there's only one thing to do: preserve it! Whether you're making tangy apricot jam or pickled summer peppers, thick apple butter or chunky tomato chutney, the process connects you to a particular time and place. Nowadays, preserving is no longer a household necessity, of course, but putting up a season's bounty— and a season's flavors—to carry you through the year still evokes a welcome nostalgia for the past. It's also a wonderfully creative and satisfying activity for nearly everyone, from the experienced cook to the kitchen novice.

Here, we've collected some of our favorite recipes for jams, jellies, marmalades, pickles, chutneys, relishes, and more, along with dozens of recipes for using them. You'll find everything from berry jam to zucchini relish, fig preserves to pickled asparagus, plus lots of variations, that will become staples in your pantry. Because together we have many years of experience, and have even won a culinary award or two, we've also shared our expertise through tips and helpful hints. Once you start thinking in terms of preserving, you'll find the options are nearly limitless. With this book as your guide, we hope you'll come to enjoy preserving as much as we do.

The Basics of Home Canning

The term "home canning," despite the implied use of cans, refers to preserving foods in specially designed glass jars. An age–old art, preserving allows you to capture the essence of fruits and vegetables at their flavorful prime—and enjoy that freshness year–round.

To make them safe for long-term shelf storage, jars of high-acid foods, like the fruit preserves and pickled vegetables featured in this book, should be processed in a boiling-water canner. Boiling the filled jars in boiling water eliminates potential contaminants and establishes a tight seal so new contaminants can't be introduced.

EQUIPMENT

Most of the basic tools and equipment you'll need to get started can be found in the housewares section of supermarkets or in kitchen-supply stores. Home-canning kits usually include a large canning pot fitted with a metal jar rack, a cover for the pot, a funnel for filling jars, a magnetic lid wand, a jar lifter, and a spatula.

Boiling-Water Canner

Using a boiling-water canner is the best way to ensure jars are sealed safely. Commonly made of porcelain-coated steel or aluminum, each canner comes with a tight-fitting lid and a removable metal rack. The rack usually holds up to seven 1-pint (16–fl oz/500-ml) jars and allows an even flow of boiling water around the jars. It sits low enough in the canner so that the tops of the jars can be covered by at least 2 inches (5 cm) of water. Handles allow you to lower the jar-filled rack into the water and secure the rack to the rim of the pot.

Home-Canning Jars

Jars specifically designed for canning foods are the safest to use, and Mason jars are the most common. Each jar is covered with a two-piece dome cap: a self-sealing lid and a metal screw band that secures the lid to the jar. Any jar that is in good condition with no cracks or chips can be used repeatedly. Screw bands can also be reused, but lids must be replaced after each use. Lids are both purchased with the jars and sold separately in packs of twelve. Jars are available with regular or wide-mouthed openings in three sizes: ½ pint (8 fl oz/ 250 ml), 1 pint (16 fl oz/500 ml), and 1 quart (1 l).

Canning Utensils

A jar lifter, resembling large tongs, has a rubber-coated clamp that securely grasps jars under the rims so the jars can be safely lowered into and lifted out of boiling water. A widemouthed funnel allows the jars to be filled neatly, with minimal spillage. A magnetic lid wand or nonmetallic tongs assist in removing the metal jar lids from the simmering water used to sterilize them. A thin nonmetallic spatula or plastic chopsticks are useful for running around the inside edge of filled jars to release air bubbles. A jelly bag, which is typically made from cheesecloth (muslin) or other porous material and is suspended from a simple metal frame, is essential for straining fruit juice for jelly.

The Basics of Fruit Spreads

Making fruit spreads—jams, jellies, preserves, conserves, marmalades—allows the home cook to capture the flavor of a favorite fruit in a jar. You need only a handful of ingredients: a sweetener, an acid, and, of course, first-rate fruit at the peak of its season.

The best fruit spreads call for balancing just a few basic ingredients. Here are some guidelines and the key elements needed for making them at home.

Fruit

Fruit spreads are only as good as the fruit you use to make them, so always seek out the most flavorful seasonal fruits. Unless you have fruit trees in your yard, farmers' markets are usually the best source. There, you can sample before you buy and ask growers when different varieties will be available. Market vendors will also often sell off-grade fruits—small fruits or fruits with cosmetic imperfections—for a reduced price. Pass up overripe fruits. Underripe fruits contain more pectin and acid, which you need for making fruit spreads, but they can also be less flavorful. For the best balance of flavor and consistency, combine slightly underripe and just-ripe fruits.

When you shop at farmers' markets, you also avoid waxed fruits. Most commercially sold apples, pears, and citrus fruits are waxed to protect them from moisture and mold during shipping and storage. Because the wax coating is not easy to remove, you must often peel the fruits before preserving them. When you peel apples and pears, you squander the valuable pectin in their skins. And if you peel citrus fruits, you lose the flavorful peel essential to a marmalade.

Pectin

Pectin is a natural carbohydrate that's concentrated in the skin and seeds of fruit. When combined with the proper ratio of sugar and acid, it causes liquids to jell. Pectin levels vary greatly among different kinds of fruits, and also within a single type of fruit depending on ripeness: the pectin diminishes as the fruit matures. Apples and citrus fruits are high in pectin and are used as the base for many packaged pectins.

Most of the recipes in this book take advantage of the pectin naturally present in the fruits, but you can also use packaged pectin to make jams, jellies, and other fruit spreads. Commercial pectin is commonly available in three types: powdered, liquid, and powdered low- or no-sugar pectin (also called low-methoxyl pectin). With all of the types, follow the package directions to ensure the fruit spread sets. Adding pectin shortens the cooking time, ensuring a fresher fruit flavor. However, even low- or no-sugar pectin needs considerable sugar or artificial sweeteners to jell the spread. You can also make your own pectin from slightly underripe apples (see page 231). Even homemade pectin calls for a generous measure of sugar to achieve the proper balance of sugar, acid, and pectin. How much pectin and sugar you'll need for a fruit spread depends on the natural pectin content of the fruit you are using (see page 230).

Sweeteners

All fruits contain sugar, but extra sugar is needed in preserves to activate the natural pectin in the fruit or the added pectin. Refined white (granulated) sugar is the most common sweetener for fruit preserves because it imparts little flavor and thus will not overpower the flavor of the fruit. Most of the recipes in this book call for this type of sugar. You can substitute organic sugar or evaporated cane juice. Some recipes, such as Pear-Ginger Jam (page 45), use brown sugar for its subtle caramel flavor. Don't substitute honey, maple or other syrups, or artificial sweeteners for the sugar in the recipes. Their flavor is too strong.

Acid

A balance of acid and sugar in fruit spreads ensures not only a good set but also a pleasing flavor. Lemon juice works well in most recipes; use Lisbon or Eureka lemons, the most common varieties (Meyer lemons have lower acid). Too much lemon juice can interfere with the flavor of the fruit. As a rule, ¼ cup (2 fl oz/60 ml) lemon juice per 1 lb (500 g) fruit works well, but taste your jam or other preserve to see if it needs more. Citric acid, or a combination of citric and ascorbic acid, can also be substituted for lemon juice. Both are available in health-food stores in crystallized form.

Flavorings

Fresh, flavorful herbs and spices—from rosemary to rosehips—can add layers of nuanced depth to your fruit spreads. Take care not to add too much, or you'll risk overpowering the fruit.

Fruit spreads by definition

Although known by various names and descriptions, here are the most commonly used terms for fruit spreads.

Conserve Usually a combination of two or more fruits, often including dried fruits and or nuts, cooked with sugar. Conserves are generally chunky.

Fruit Butter Puréed fruit cooked slowly with a little sugar until the liquid evaporates and the mixture becomes dark and thick.

Jam Chopped, crushed, or mashed fruit cooked with sugar (and sometimes with added pectin). The set, or firmness, of the finished jam varies depending on the cook's preference and the pectin content of the fruit. The best jams are made with fruits that have medium to high levels of natural pectin.

Jelly Jelled fruit juice with added sugar (and pectin, if needed). A perfect jelly should be clear and should jiggle when touched, and never be rubbery. Jellies do not contain any pieces of fruit or peel. Some jellies are made with savory ingredients, like vegetables or herbs, and added pectin.

Marmalade Chopped, puréed, or sliced citrus peel—either one type or a mixture from different fruits—cooked with sugar. The soft, cooked peel is suspended in a jelly made from the fruit juice.

Preserves Whole cooked fruits or fruit pieces suspended in a soft jelly or syrup. Preserves often include spices, wine, or spirits and are typically made from fruits that have little natural pectin, or that would otherwise require time-consuming processing, such as cherries, which must be pitted for jam or other spreads. "Preserves" is also a common term for all fruit spreads.

TIPS FROM A PRESERVING PRO

It can be frustrating to spend money and time preserving fruits, only to produce a batch that doesn't turn out as you had hoped. These tips can be lifesavers:

Make small batches

With small batches, you have better control over heat levels, and if something goes wrong, you haven't wasted too much time or fruit. Small batches also cook faster, so you'll preserve the fresh flavor of the fruit better.

Know your fruit

Most of the recipes in this book do not call for commercial pectin. Refer to the chart on page 230 to find the amount of natural pectin the fruit you're using contains, and adjust your expectations and cooking times accordingly.

Start with jam

For the novice preserver, jam is the place to begin: it requires little fruit preparation and is forgiving. Even if your jam doesn't set firmly, it will still taste delicious.

Have special equipment handy

In addition to the equipment recommended on page 8, it's useful to have two large nonreactive spoons (one slotted and one not) and a large ladle. A sturdy pair of clean rubber garden gloves lets you hold the filled, hot jars securely so you can give them a good, firm twist.

Choose the right pan

Cook jams and other fruit spreads in a wide, shallow nonreactive pan. The wider surface area ensures any liquid will evaporate quickly, so you won't have to overcook the fruit, which can result in a caramel taste and runny consistency.

Taste and adjust

The balance of acid and sugar is important to the final flavor. Follow the recipes precisely, then taste as your fruit spread cooks and adjust as needed. Be careful not to add too much lemon juice; it can impart an overpowering flavor.

Cook gently

Most of the recipes in this book call for cooking over medium-high heat. Don't boil your preserves too hard, as doing so can cause the sugar to crystallize and the natural pectin to evaporate.

Don't overcook

Fruit needs to be cooked in order to exude pectin, but if you cook it for too long, you can cook the pectin right out of the fruit and end up with runny preserves. Overcooking can also result in a burnt flavor. Follow recipe instructions for the best results, watching and stirring to avoid scorching.

Use the correct headspace

If the top of your fruit spread darkens, it's usually because you left too much space between the fruit and the lid, or headspace, when you filled the jar (see page 228). The darkening does not indicate spoilage, however, so you can still eat the preserves; just skim off and discard the top layer.

Store jars carefully

Exposure to sunlight, or a storage area that is too warm, can cause fruit spreads to lose their color, flavor, and texture. Store fruit spreads for no more than a year in a cool, dark place.

The Basics of Pickling

Preserving foods through pickling dates back more than four millennia. Over the centuries, it has emerged in numerous cultures around the world and taken a wide range of forms. The impetus to pickle came from a common goal: to preserve for future consumption.

Nowadays, the technique is still used to capture harvest's bounty and ensure ample food for winter. But pickles are also made for the simple reason that they are delicious. Here are some guidelines for pickling at home, and the key elements involved.

Produce

An easy way to think about handling produce for pickling is to remember the two Fs: fresh and fast. Produce pickled at its peak of freshness will invariably yield the best result. In terms of taste, it's clear why this is true. The freshest produce will also have the crispiest texture, necessary for a good pickle. For this reason, avoid vegetables with blemishes or soft areas. Fast is equally important. Make your pickles as soon as possible after picking or sourcing your produce. Don't let foods sit in the kitchen and soften. Maintaining the integrity of the vegetables is an important factor in controlling the pickling process.

Salt

Salt is a key ingredient in a wide range of pickling methods. In many brines, salt tempers the balance of flavors, as it also does when you add salt to food at the table. In some cases, salt helps draw water out of vegetables, such as cucumbers, to improve their texture. Kosher salt and pickling salt, which are nearly identical, are the two main types of salt used for making shelf-stable pickles. Do not substitute common table salt. Some people add a lot of salt to brines in order to achieve an actual salty flavor—but the subtleties of spices, herbs, and citrus will generate more distinctive and nuanced final results.

Acid

Acids are a vital element in making shelf-stable pickles. Properly sealed jars of pickles can remain on the shelf for a long period of time because they have achieved an acceptable level of acidification, the pH of the contents (pickles and brine) has been stabilized, and all bacteria have been eradicated.

Acid in pickling takes two forms: vinegar and citric acid. Vinegar, an acetic acid, works on pickled vegetables to stabilize their pH levels. Different vinegars have different degrees of strength, or grain. Most vinegars commonly used in pickling have a grain strength of 5 or 6 percent. Avoid using vinegars with a grain strength lower than what the recipe requires, as this may result in pickles that don't acidify properly. Citric acid takes the form of juice from citrus: lemon, lime, and orange. It brightens and embellishes the flavors of pickles and complements other ingredients, but it doesn't usually provide the basis for acidification.

Heat penetration is another factor in acidification. Brines are brought to a boil (212°F/100°C) and poured quickly into jars before their temperature drops below 195°F (91°C), which typically takes a few minutes. Jars remain in the boiling-water bath for a specified length of time to ensure that the core temperature—the temperature at the middle—of the contents reaches a level that will kill any form of bacteria present.

The combination of vinegar and heat penetration will reliably kill bacteria, and if jars have been properly sealed, the contents are safe to eat. Many first-time picklers are nervous about making pickles, fearing that they may not be safe to consume. By following the simple instructions in this book, you can proceed with confidence.

Herbs & Spices

Different combinations of herbs and spices help create pickles with distinctive flavors, and experimenting with these elements is where you can make your mark as a pickler. As you gain confidence, alter recipes to suit your tastes. For instance, for recipes that call for chiles and other heat-producing ingredients, what's spicy to one person's palate is often mild to another's. There is no right or wrong. Just remember to record your modifications so that when you hit on something you like, you can easily do it again. Coming off the vine, a cucumber is a cucumber. What you do with it from there makes your creations special, and herbs and spices are your allies in this process.

A general note: A little often goes a long way. Start with less than you might think you need to avoid overwhelming the rest of the ingredients.

The power of pickling spice

The combination of a vegetable (or fruit), a vinegar, and pickling spice comprise the pickler's palette. But it is perhaps the pickling spice—the unique and flavorful mix of herbs and spices added to the brine—that plays the most creative and distinctive role.

Pickling spice is a bit like barbecue sauce; everyone has a personal style and preference of taste. You can purchase pickling spice blends at the store, or make your own. For an aromatic approach, you might include as many as 6 or 8 spices—such as whole allspice, peppercorns, dill and mustard seeds, and bay leaves. Try experimenting with different flavor profiles, and be sure to log all of the combinations you try. Whatever aromatic notes you find appealing, increase; those that seem as if they are interfering, decrease. The recipe below is a good starting point.

Homemade Pickling Spice

1 cinnamon stick, broken into pieces

2 dried bay leaves, crushed

2 whole cloves

2 Tbsp mustard seeds

2 Tbsp whole coriander seeds

1 Tbsp mixed peppercorns

2 tsp whole allspice

2 tsp dill seeds

1 tsp red pepper flakes

Combine all of the ingredients in a small bowl. Store in an airtight container at room temperature for up to 1 year.

TIPS FROM A PICKLING PRO

For aspiring and experienced picklers alike, the following pointers offer helpful advice for every step of the pickling process:

Start with a clean and tidy work area

You'll be handling materials at high temperatures, and you'll want to be able to move them where they need to go quickly and easily.

Don't forget the two Fs: fresh and fast

The best pickles are made with produce picked that day or the day before. Strive to shorten the amount of time between when you pick or purchase produce and when you pickle it. Even under refrigeration, vegetables lose structure and texture, and no one likes a soft pickle.

Use aromatic spices and herbs

If you're planning a series of canning sessions, make sure your seasonings are stored in airtight containers from one session to the next.

Measure ingredients carefully

Let's say you're making a pickle that calls for adding 1 teaspoon cayenne pepper. There's a big difference between a level teaspoon and a heaping teaspoon, and this difference will play out even more as the finished, sealed jars rest and the ingredients mingle and their flavors develop.

Resist overpacking your jars

While it can be tempting to do so, don't overpack your jars. Depending on which vegetables you're pickling, jamming too many into a jar can create a situation where you won't be able to extract the contents once the jar is processed because the vegetables are so tightly packed. Additionally, pasteurizing depends on brine circulation, so you'll want to leave enough space for the brine to move freely in the jar.

Take your time with the brine

When adding the brine, pour to the fill line, then agitate the jar, shaking it laterally, to let the brine settle—then top it off if necessary. Make sure to top off the brine, cap the jars, and start to process within 5 minutes.

Don't multitask while processing

When you're pickling, a certain amount of multitasking goes on—you might be packing jars while simmering the brine. But when it comes to processing, focus on the timing. If your processing time is off by a few seconds, don't fret. Just keep in mind that timing is specific for a reason.

Pickling is a handmade process

Even as you strive for consistency and work toward making the best possible pickle, it's natural and normal for batches to be slightly different from one to the next.

There are no bad pickling experiments

Trial and error is the best way to expand your repertoire. Have fun with it and don't forget that you can pickle almost anything.

Think of your pickles as works of art

Finished pickles will draw gratitude and enthusiastic compliments from your friends as they examine the vegetables, herbs, and spices artfully arranged inside the jars. You'll soon discover that bringing a jar of homemade pickles to a party as a gift is greatly appreciated.

JAMS & JELLIES

"Preserving connects you to a particular place and moment in time, whether it's the memory of a sunny afternoon spent picking strawberries or the scent of warm peaches simmering on a summer morning."

REBECCA COURCHESNE

STRAWBERRIES • RASPBERRIES • PLUMS • GRAPES • PEACHES • APRICOTS

Jams are straightforward: cut-up or crushed fruit is combined with sugar and lemon juice and heated to activate the fruit's natural pectin, which is what makes the mixture jell. The best jams are brightly colored and flavored and have a soft consistency that spreads easily. Berries—especially strawberries and raspberries—are the rock stars of the jam world, but stone fruits like apricots, peaches, and plums are popular players, too.

Jellies are clear, shimmering, and packed with flavor. Like jams, they call for combining fruit with sugar and an acid, and heating the mix. But then they go their separate ways. Jelly mixtures are strained through the fine weave of a jelly bag, yielding a perfectly clear liquid that sets up beautifully, usually thanks to some additional pectin. Good jellies quiver slightly when jostled and hold their shape when cut. They can be made from sweet, savory, or hot ingredients, such as grapes, apples, pomegranates, mint, kiwifruits, chiles, and citrus.

In the kitchen and at the table, jams and jellies are used much the same way: in cookies, layer cakes, and parfaits; as glazes for meats or poultry; and slathered on scones, muffins, and toast.

You can experiment with the ratio of berries in this recipe and, if you like, substitute 2 cups (½ lb/250 g) hulled and halved strawberries for 2 cups (½ lb/250 g) of the raspberries. The blackberries and blueberries give the jam lots of body as well as an intense berry flavor.

Mixed Berry Jam

Have ready hot, sterilized jars and their lids (see page 228).

In a large nonreactive saucepan, gently toss together the berries, sugar, and lemon juice. Bring to a boil over medium-high heat, reduce the heat to medium, and cook, uncovered, stirring frequently, until the jam has thickened, about 15 minutes. It will continue to thicken as it cools.

Ladle the hot jam into the jars, leaving ¼ inch (6 mm) of headspace. Remove any air bubbles and adjust the headspace, if necessary. Wipe the rims clean and seal tightly with the lids.

Process the jars for 10 minutes in a boiling-water bath (for detailed instructions, including cooling and testing seals, see pages 228–229). The sealed jars can be stored in a cool, dark place for up to 1 year. If a seal has failed, store the jar in the refrigerator for up to 1 month.

4 cups (1 lb/500 g) raspberries

4 cups (1 lb/500 g) blackberries

4 cups (1 lb/500 g) blueberries

3 cups (1½ lb/750 g) sugar

¾ cup (6 fl oz/180 ml) fresh lemon juice

Makes 6 half-pint (8–fl oz/250-ml) jars

This is a classic summer jam, full of great berry flavor. Make several batches throughout raspberry season—you'll want to put it on everything from pancakes to muffins to sandwiches. It's also perfect for layer cakes (page 29) and thumbprint cookies (page 33).

Raspberry Jam

In a large nonreactive bowl, gently toss together the raspberries and sugar. Cover and let stand at room temperature for 2–4 hours.

Have ready hot, sterilized jars and their lids (see page 228). Place 2 or 3 small plates in the freezer.

Transfer the raspberry mixture to a large nonreactive saucepan and add the lemon juice. Bring to a boil over medium-high heat, reduce the heat to medium, and cook, uncovered, stirring frequently, for 10 minutes. Remove from the heat. Use 1 tsp jam and a chilled plate to test if the jam is ready (see page 231).

Ladle the hot jam into the jars, leaving ¼ inch (6 mm) of headspace. Remove any air bubbles and adjust the headspace, if necessary. Wipe the rims clean and seal tightly with the lids.

Process the jars for 10 minutes in a boiling-water bath (for detailed instructions, including cooling and testing seals, see pages 228–229). The sealed jars can be stored in a cool, dark place for up to 1 year. If a seal has failed, store the jar in the refrigerator for up to 1 month.

9 cups (2¼ lb/1.12 kg) raspberries

2½ cups (1¼ lb/625 g) sugar

½ cup (4 fl oz/125 ml) fresh lemon juice

Makes 7 or 8 half-pint (8–fl oz/250-ml) jars

Raspberry–Rose Geranium Jam
If your garden has a rose geranium, pick 10 small or 6 large leaves with stems. Securely tie them together with kitchen string and simmer them with the fruit mixture. Taste the jam occasionally until it has the desired rose scent and remove the bag.

This luscious cake is ideal for birthdays, showers, or garden parties. You can also use this basic recipe to make a lemon curd layer cake, using Lemon Curd (page 109) in place of the jam filling and the icing. You'll need about 2 cups (16 fl oz/500 ml) of curd.

Coconut-Raspberry Layer Cake

Preheat the oven to 350°F (180°C). Butter two 9-inch (23-cm) round cake pans, line with waxed paper, and butter and flour the paper.

In a bowl, sift together the flour, baking powder, and salt. In another bowl, using an electric mixer on medium-high speed, beat the butter until light. Gradually beat in the sugar. Add the egg yolks, one at a time. Add the flour mixture in three batches alternating with the milk in two batches. Beat in the vanilla. In a large bowl, using an electric mixer and clean beaters, beat the egg whites until stiff peaks form. Fold the whites into the batter, then divide between the prepared pans.

Bake until a toothpick inserted in the center of a cake comes out clean, about 30 minutes. Let cool in the pans on wire racks for 5 minutes, then invert onto the racks, remove the paper, and let cool.

To make the icing, in a saucepan over low heat, stir the sugar, salt, and ⅔ cup (5 fl oz/160 ml) water until the sugar dissolves. Raise the heat to medium-high, bring to a rolling boil, and boil until the syrup registers 240°F (115°C) on a candy thermometer. Set aside.

In a bowl, using an electric mixer on medium-high speed, beat the egg whites until soft peaks form. Raise the speed to high, add the syrup in a thin stream, and beat until thick and glossy, about 7 minutes. Beat in the vanilla.

On a serving plate, spread the jam evenly on the bottom cake layer, and top with the second layer. Cover the top and sides of the cake with the icing, and then the coconut. Refrigerate until serving.

3 cups (12 oz/375 g) cake (soft-wheat) flour

1 Tbsp baking powder

½ tsp salt

½ cup (4 oz/125 g) unsalted butter, at room temperature

1¼ cups (10 oz/315 g) sugar

3 eggs, separated

1⅓ cups (11 fl oz/340 ml) milk

2 tsp pure vanilla extract

¾ cup (7½ oz/235 g) Raspberry Jam (facing page)

3 cups (9 oz/270 g) sweetened flaked coconut

FOR THE ICING

1⅓ cups (11 oz/345 g) sugar

⅛ tsp salt

4 egg whites

1 tsp pure vanilla extract

Serves 10–12

A bowl of plain yogurt is made extra special with a swirl of berry jam and a sprinkle of homemade granola. You can tailor the granola recipe to your liking, such as substituting sunflower seeds or chopped pecans for the almonds and dried cranberries for the cherries.

Yogurt Parfaits with Berry Jam & Granola

To make the granola, preheat the oven to 300°F (150°C). Line a rimmed baking sheet with parchment (baking) paper.

In a large bowl, combine the oats, almonds, coconut, brown sugar, and salt. In a small saucepan over low heat, combine the honey and oil and heat, stirring, until hot. Drizzle the honey mixture over the oat mixture and stir to coat evenly. Spread the mixture on the prepared sheet, leaving small clumps of oats.

Bake, stirring occasionally, until the granola is golden brown, about 30 minutes. Let the granola cool completely on the pan on a wire rack. Stir in the dried cherries.

To assemble the parfaits, place ¼ cup (2 oz/60 g) yogurt in the bottom of each of 4 glasses or bowls. Spread 2 Tbsp of the jam gently over the yogurt and then sprinkle with granola to taste. (Store leftover granola in an airtight container at room temperature for up to 1 week.) Top with the remaining yogurt, garnish with berries and serve at once.

FOR THE GRANOLA

2 cups (6 oz/185 g) old-fashioned rolled oats

⅓ cup (1½ oz/45 g) slivered blanched almonds

⅓ cup (1½ oz/45 g) shredded coconut

1 Tbsp firmly packed light brown sugar

¼ tsp salt

¼ cup (3 oz/90 g) honey

2 Tbsp canola oil

⅓ cup (1½ oz/45 g) dried pitted cherries or raisins

2 cups (1 lb/500 g) Greek-style plain yogurt

½ cup (5 oz/155 g) Mixed Berry Jam (page 27) or other berry jam

Berries for garnish

Serves 4

The optional addition of apricot kernels adds a mellow almond flavor to this jam. Roasting the pits makes them easier to crack open, and roasting the kernels makes them safe to eat. Spread the jam on toast, spoon it into thumbprint cookies, or use it as a glaze for meat.

Apricot Jam

Halve and pit the apricots, reserving 10 pits for later use, if desired. Slice the apricots. In a large nonreactive bowl, gently toss together the apricots and sugar. Cover and let stand at room temperature for at least 4 hours or up to overnight in the refrigerator.

Meanwhile, if using the apricot kernels, roast the pits, remove the kernels, and roast the kernels (see page 234).

Have ready hot, sterilized jars and their lids (see page 228).

Transfer the apricot mixture to a large nonreactive saucepan and add the lemon juice. Bring to a simmer over medium-low heat and cook, uncovered, stirring frequently, until most of the liquid has evaporated and the jam is thick, 15–20 minutes.

Drop 2 roasted apricot kernels, if using, into each jar. Ladle the hot jam into the jars, leaving ¼ inch (6 mm) of headspace. Remove any air bubbles and adjust the headspace, if necessary. Wipe the rims clean and seal tightly with the lids.

Process the jars for 10 minutes in a boiling-water bath (for detailed instructions, including cooling and testing seals, see pages 228–229). The sealed jars can be stored in a cool, dark place for up to 1 year. If a seal has failed, store the jar in the refrigerator for up to 1 month.

3 lb (1.5 kg) apricots

2 cups (1 lb/500 g) sugar

½ cup (4 fl oz/125 ml) fresh lemon juice

Makes 5 half-pint (8–fl oz/250-ml) jars

These small cookies are irresistible, and children will be happy to help you make them by forming small thumbprints in the dough. Filling half of the cookies with one type of jam and half with another type adds attractive and colorful contrast to a plate of these popular sweets.

Pecan-Apricot Thumbprint Cookies

Preheat the oven to 350°F (180°C).

In a small bowl, sift together the flour and salt. In a large bowl, using an electric mixer on high speed, beat the butter, brown sugar, and vanilla until light and fluffy. Beat in the egg yolk. Reduce the speed to low. Add the flour mixture and pecans, and mix until just incorporated.

Roll pieces of the dough between your palms to form 1-inch (2.5-cm) balls. Arrange them on an ungreased baking sheet, spacing them about 1½ inches (4 cm) apart. Using your thumbs, make a depression about ¼ inch (6 mm) deep in the center of each ball.

Bake the cookies for 10 minutes. Fill the depressions in the cookies with the jam. Continue baking the cookies until they begin to color, about 10 minutes longer. Transfer the cookies to wire racks to cool. Store in an airtight container at room temperature for up to 5 days.

1 cup (5 oz/155 g) all-purpose (plain) flour

⅛ tsp salt

½ cup (4 oz/125 g) unsalted butter, at room temperature

⅓ cup (2½ oz/75 g) firmly packed light brown sugar

¾ tsp pure vanilla extract

1 egg yolk

¾ cup (3 oz/90 g) pecans, coarsely ground

½ cup (5 oz/155 g) Apricot Jam (facing page) or other fruit jam

Makes about 2 dozen cookies

Strawberries and rhubarb are the long-awaited first sign of spring fruit. Because both are low in pectin, oranges, both the peel and the flesh, are added to give this bright-flavored, tangy jam the body it needs. Set it out with cream scones, biscuits, or crusty bread.

Strawberry-Rhubarb Jam

Cut the ends off each orange. Cut the oranges in half crosswise and remove the seeds. Place the orange halves in a food processor and process until roughly puréed. Transfer to a nonreactive bowl. Add the rhubarb, strawberries, and sugar and toss gently to combine. Cover and refrigerate for at least 8 hours or up to overnight.

The next day, have ready hot, sterilized jars and their lids (see page 228). Place 2 or 3 small plates in the freezer.

Transfer the rhubarb mixture to a large nonreactive saucepan and add the lemon juice. Bring to a boil over medium-high heat, reduce the heat to medium, and cook, uncovered, stirring frequently, for 10 minutes. Remove from the heat. Use 1 tsp jam and a chilled plate to test if the jam is ready (see page 231).

Ladle the hot jam into the jars, leaving ¼ inch (6 mm) of headspace. Remove any air bubbles and adjust the headspace, if necessary. Wipe the rims clean and seal tightly with the lids.

Process the jars for 10 minutes in a boiling-water bath (for detailed instructions, including cooling and testing seals, see pages 228–229). The sealed jars can be stored in a cool, dark place for up to 1 year. If a seal has failed, store the jar in the refrigerator for up to 1 month.

2 oranges, preferably blood oranges

1½–2 lb (750 g–1 kg) rhubarb, cut into ½-inch (12-mm) chunks (about 6 cups)

3 cups (¾ lb/375 g) strawberries, hulled and sliced

4 cups (2 lb/1 kg) sugar

½ cup (4 fl oz/125 ml) fresh lemon juice

Makes 7 half-pint (8-fl oz/250-ml) jars

This vibrant jam goes well with sweet or savory dishes: spoon it over vanilla ice cream or use it to deglaze a pan after cooking pork chops. Plums call for more sugar than other stone fruits because of their bitter skin, which contains much of the plum flavor and pectin.

Plum Jam

In a large nonreactive bowl, gently toss together the plums and sugar. Cover and let stand at room temperature for at least 4 hours or up to overnight in the refrigerator.

Have ready hot, sterilized jars and their lids (see page 228). Place 2 or 3 small plates in the freezer.

Transfer the plum mixture to a large nonreactive saucepan and add the lemon juice. Bring to a boil over medium-high heat, reduce the heat to medium, and cook, uncovered, stirring frequently, for 10 minutes. Remove from the heat. Use 1 tsp jam and a chilled plate to test if the jam is ready (see page 231).

Ladle the hot jam into the jars, leaving ¼ inch (6 mm) of headspace. Remove any air bubbles and adjust the headspace, if necessary. Wipe the rims clean and seal tightly with the lids.

Process the jars for 10 minutes in a boiling-water bath (for detailed instructions, including cooling and testing seals, see pages 228–229). The sealed jars can be stored in a cool, dark place for up to 1 year. If a seal has failed, store the jar in the refrigerator for up to 1 month.

2½–3 lb (1.25–1.5 kg) plums such as Santa Rosa or pluots such as Flavor King, halved, pitted, and quartered (about 8 cups)

3 cups (1½ lb/750 g) sugar

½ cup (4 oz/125 ml) fresh lemon juice

Makes 6 half-pint (8–fl oz/250-ml) jars

Plum-Lavender Jam
Place 1 tsp dried lavender flowers on a square of cheesecloth (muslin). Bring the corners together and tie securely with kitchen string. Add to the plum mixture just after it begins to simmer. Taste the jam as it cooks and remove the bag when the desired lavender flavor is achieved.

Cherries help give body and extra sweetness to this classic jam. For a variation, use balsamic vinegar, which offers depth of flavor without being overly assertive. A true 14-year-old balsamic is best; younger vinegars will work, but can be very acidic, so don't add too much.

Strawberry Jam

In a large nonreactive bowl, gently toss together the strawberries, cherries, and sugar. Cover and let stand at room temperature for 1–2 hours.

Have ready hot, sterilized jars and their lids (see page 228). Place 2 or 3 small plates in the freezer.

Transfer the fruit mixture to a large nonreactive saucepan and add the lemon juice. Bring to a boil over medium-high heat, reduce the heat to medium, and cook, uncovered, stirring frequently, for 10 minutes. Remove from the heat. Use 1 tsp jam and a chilled plate to test if the jam is ready (see page 231).

Ladle the hot jam into the jars, leaving ¼ inch (6 mm) of headspace. Remove any air bubbles and adjust the headspace, if necessary. Wipe the rims clean and seal tightly with the lids.

Process the jars for 10 minutes in a boiling-water bath (for detailed instructions, including cooling and testing seals, see pages 228–229). The sealed jars can be stored in a cool, dark place for up to 1 year. If a seal has failed, store the jar in the refrigerator for up to 1 month.

8 cups (2 lb/1 kg) strawberries, hulled and halved

2 lb (1 kg) cherries, pitted and roughly chopped

2½ cups (1¼ lb/625 g) sugar

½ cup (4 fl oz/125 ml) fresh lemon juice

Makes 6 half-pint (8–fl oz/250-ml) jars

Strawberry-Balsamic Jam
Add ¼ cup (2 fl oz/60 ml) balsamic vinegar during the last 3–4 minutes of cooking the fruit mixture. Be careful not to overcook it, or the jam will take on a caramelized flavor.

Here, delicate, butter-rich cookies sandwich strawberry jam for a teatime treat. For an even prettier presentation, use a second, smaller cookie cutter to cut a window in the top of each cookie before baking to allow the colorful jam to show. You can use any flavor of fruit jam.

Strawberry Jam Sandwich Cookies

In a bowl, sift together the flour, cornstarch, and salt. In another bowl, using an electric mixer on high speed, beat the butter and zest until light. Add the granulated sugar and beat until completely incorporated. Add the whole egg and egg yolk and beat until light and fluffy. Reduce the speed to low, add the flour mixture, and beat until just incorporated. Gather the dough into a ball and divide into thirds. Flatten each third into a disk. Wrap separately in waxed paper and refrigerate for at least 1 hour or up to overnight.

Preheat the oven to 350°F (180°C). Lightly grease baking sheets.

Dust 1 dough disk with flour and place between 2 large sheets of waxed paper. Roll out the dough ⅛ inch (3 mm) thick. Using a 3-inch (7.5-cm) decoratively shaped cutter, cut out cookies. Transfer the cookies to the prepared baking sheets, spacing them about ½ inch (12 mm) apart. Refrigerate for 10 minutes. Gather the dough scraps into a ball, wrap in waxed paper, and refrigerate.

Bake until the edges of the cookies are golden, about 10 minutes. Transfer to wire racks to cool. Repeat with the remaining 2 disks, then roll out, cut, chill, and bake the scraps in the same manner.

Spread the jam on the bottoms of half of the cookies, spreading it lightly at the edges. Top with the remaining cookies, bottoms down. Dust the tops with confectioners' sugar, if desired. Store in an airtight container in the refrigerator for up to 1 week.

2¼ cups (11½ oz/360 g) all-purpose (plain) flour

¼ cup (1 oz/30 g) cornstarch (cornflour)

¼ tsp salt

¾ cup (6 oz/185 g) unsalted butter, at room temperature

1½ tsp grated lemon zest

1 cup (8 oz/250 g) granulated sugar

1 whole egg plus 1 egg yolk

About 2 cups (1¼ lb/ 625 g) Strawberry Jam (page 37) or other fruit jam

Confectioners' (icing) sugar for dusting (optional)

Makes about 3 dozen cookies

The last blueberries of the season just barely overlap with the arrival of the first plums. It's worth saving some blueberries to make this slightly tart jam. Any type of plum will do here, from small, golden-fleshed Damsons to the sweeter Santa Rosa and Satsuma varieties.

Blueberry-Plum Jam

In a large nonreactive bowl, gently toss together the plums, blueberries, and sugar. Cover and let stand at room temperature for 2–4 hours or up to overnight in the refrigerator.

Have ready hot, sterilized jars and their lids (see page 228). Place 2 or 3 small plates in the freezer.

Transfer the plum mixture to a large nonreactive saucepan and add the lemon juice. Bring to a boil over medium-high heat, reduce the heat to medium, and cook, uncovered, stirring frequently, for 10 minutes. Remove from the heat. Use 1 tsp jam and a chilled plate to test if the jam is ready (see page 231).

Ladle the hot jam into the jars, leaving ¼ inch (6 mm) of headspace. Remove any air bubbles and adjust the headspace, if necessary. Wipe the rims clean and seal tightly with the lids.

Process the jars for 10 minutes in a boiling-water bath (for detailed instructions, including cooling and testing seals, see pages 228–229). The sealed jars can be stored in a cool, dark place for up to 1 year. If a seal has failed, store the jar in the refrigerator for up to 1 month.

2½ lb (1.25 kg) plums, halved, pitted, and sliced (about 8 cups)

3 cups (¾ lb/375 g) blueberries

2 cups (1 lb/500 g) sugar

½ cup (4 fl oz/125 ml) fresh lemon juice

Makes 7 or 8 half-pint (8–fl oz/250-ml) jars

These jam–filled pastries are a breeze to make and a pleasure to eat. Serve for dessert with a scoop of ice cream, or for breakfast with an assortment of pastries. You can use any flavor of jam you like, or, try replacing 1 Tbsp of the jam filling with cream cheese.

Blueberry-Plum Jam Turnovers

Preheat the oven to 425°F (220°C). Line a baking sheet with parchment (baking) paper.

Place the puff pastry sheet on a lightly floured work surface and roll out into a 15-by-10-inch (38-by-25-cm) rectangle. Cut the rectangle in half lengthwise and then cut each half crosswise into 3 squares. Place the squares on the prepared baking sheet.

In a small bowl, whisk together the egg and milk. Brush a ½-inch (12-mm) border of the egg mixture around 2 adjacent sides of each pastry square. Spoon 2½–3 Tbsp of the jam almost in the middle of the square. Fold the pastry over the jam filling to make a triangle and press the edges firmly with a fork to seal. Repeat with the remaining squares. Brush the tops of the pastries with the remaining egg mixture and sprinkle with the sugar.

Bake until the turnovers are puffed and golden brown, 15–18 minutes. Let cool slightly on the baking sheet on a wire rack. Serve warm.

1 sheet frozen puff pastry, about 8½ oz (265 g), thawed according to package directions

1 egg

1 Tbsp milk

About 1 cup (10 oz/315 g) Blueberry-Plum Jam (facing page) or other fruit jam

Coarse sugar such as turbinado for sprinkling

Makes 6 turnovers

As for Apricot Jam (page 32), the kernels from the pits can be used to infuse the jam. Keeping the skins on the peaches intensifies the flavor of the jam and helps thicken it. The peaches should be ripe but not too ripe; the riper the fruit, the less pectin in the skin.

Peach Jam

Halve and pit the peaches, reserving 8 pits for later use, if desired. Cut the peaches into slices ½ inch (12 mm) thick (you should have about 12 cups). In a large nonreactive bowl, gently toss together the peaches and sugar. Cover and let stand at room temperature for at least 4 hours or up to overnight in the refrigerator.

Meanwhile, if using the peach kernels, roast the pits, remove the kernels, and roast the kernels (see page 234).

Have ready hot, sterilized jars and their lids (see page 228).

Transfer the peach mixture to a large nonreactive saucepan and add the lemon juice. Bring to a simmer over medium-low heat and cook, uncovered, stirring frequently, until most of the liquid has evaporated and the jam is thick, 10–15 minutes.

Drop 1 roasted peach kernel, if using, into each jar. Ladle the hot jam into the jars, leaving ¼ inch (6 mm) of headspace. Remove any air bubbles and adjust the headspace, if necessary. Wipe the rims clean and seal tightly with the lids.

Process the jars for 10 minutes in a boiling-water bath (for detailed instructions, including cooling and testing seals, see pages 228–229). The sealed jars can be stored in a cool, dark place for up to 1 year. If a seal has failed, store the jar in the refrigerator for up to 1 month.

5½ lb (2.75 kg) peaches, fuzz gently rubbed from the skins

3 cups (1½ lb/750 g) sugar

¾ cup (6 fl oz/180 ml) fresh lemon juice

Makes 7 or 8 half-pint (8-fl oz/250-ml) jars

This whole ham easily serves a big crowd. To serve a smaller group, purchase half of a fully cooked bone-in smoked ham and allow about 20 minutes of cooking time per pound. Decrease the glaze ingredients by half, and glaze the ham once during cooking.

Ham with Ginger-Peach Glaze

Preheat the oven to 325°F (165°C). Place a rack in a roasting pan.

Trim the fat from the ham, leaving a layer of fat about ¼ inch (6 mm) thick, then score the fat in a diamond pattern. Set the ham, fat side up, on the rack in the pan. Pour the wine into the pan and tent the ham with aluminum foil, sealing the edges securely. Bake for 2 hours.

Meanwhile, make the glaze: In a small saucepan over medium heat, stir together the jam, ginger, and mustard until the jam melts.

Remove the ham from the oven. Remove and discard the foil. Raise the oven temperature to 350°F (180°C). Stir about 2 Tbsp of the pan juices into the glaze to thin it slightly. Spoon about three-fourths of the glaze over the ham. Sprinkle 2 Tbsp of the sugar over the glaze, then pat it with the back of a spoon so that it clings to the meat. Return the ham to the oven and continue to bake for 1 hour.

Remove the ham from the oven and baste with the pan juices. Spoon the remaining glaze over the top and pat with the remaining sugar. Continue to bake until the glaze is browned and bubbly and an instant-read thermometer inserted into the thickest part of the ham away from the bone registers 160°F (71°C), about 30 minutes. Remove from the oven, tent loosely with foil, and let rest for 25 minutes.

Transfer the ham to a platter. Beginning at the large end, thinly slice across the grain. Serve hot or at room temperature.

1 fully cooked bone-in smoked ham, about 15 lb (7.5 kg)

2 cups (16 fl oz/500 ml) dry white wine

FOR THE GLAZE

1½ cups (15 oz/470 g) Peach Jam (page 42)

1½ tsp ground ginger

1 tsp dry mustard

4 Tbsp (2 oz/60 g) firmly packed light brown sugar

Serves 20–24

This autumnal jam can be used as an accompaniment to gingerbread or spooned over vanilla ice cream. The brown sugar gives it a deep caramel flavor, though you can use all granulated sugar if you like. Use young, firm fresh ginger for the brightest flavor.

Pear-Ginger Jam

Have ready hot, sterilized jars and their lids (see page 228).

In a large nonreactive saucepan, gently toss together the pears, fresh ginger, sugar, lemon juice, and crystallized ginger, if using. Bring to a boil over medium-high heat, reduce the heat to medium, and cook, uncovered, stirring frequently, until most of the liquid has evaporated and the jam is thick, about 10 minutes.

Ladle the hot jam into the jars, leaving ¼ inch (6 mm) of headspace. Remove any air bubbles and adjust the headspace, if necessary. Wipe the rims clean and seal tightly with the lids.

Process the jars for 10 minutes in a boiling-water bath (for detailed instructions, including cooling and testing seals, see pages 228–229). The sealed jars can be stored in a cool, dark place for up to 1 year. If a seal has failed, store the jar in the refrigerator for up to 1 month.

3 lb (1.5 kg) pears such as Comice or Warren, peeled, cored, and cut into ½-inch (12-mm) cubes (about 8 cups)

1 Tbsp peeled and finely grated fresh ginger

1 cup (6 oz/185 g) lightly packed light brown sugar

¼ cup (2 fl oz/60 ml) fresh lemon juice

1 Tbsp finely chopped crystallized ginger (optional)

Makes 5 half-pint (8–fl oz/250-ml) jars

This pulled pork, doused in a sweet-and-sour soaking sauce with a generous helping of peach jam, is perfect picnic fare. Serve it on a platter alongside soft sandwich rolls, sliced dill pickles (page 122), and coleslaw, allowing diners to assemble their own sandwiches.

Pulled Pork with Spicy Peach-Mustard Sauce

Preheat the oven to 300°F (150°C). Lightly oil a large baking pan.

Place the pork shoulder in the prepared pan and rub with 1 Tbsp salt, 1 Tbsp pepper, and the mustard seeds. Pour 1 cup (8 fl oz/250 ml) of the vinegar and 1 cup water over and around the pork. Scatter the sliced onions over and around the meat. Cover with aluminum foil and roast for 4 hours. Remove the foil and continue to roast until an instant-read meat thermometer inserted into the thickest part of the pork away from the bone registers 180°F (82°C) and the juices run clear, about 1 hour longer. Remove the pork from the pan and let stand for 1 hour. Using 2 forks, shred the pork, discarding any fat. Place the pork in a bowl. Using a slotted spoon, lift the roasted onions from the pan and add to the pork. Mix well to combine.

Meanwhile, in a saucepan over medium heat, melt the butter. Add the chopped onions and the garlic and cook, stirring occasionally, until the onions are soft and beginning to brown, about 10 minutes. Add the tomatoes, tomato paste, jam, mustard, bourbon, honey, brown sugar, remaining 1 cup vinegar, and hot-pepper sauce and stir to mix well. Season with salt and pepper. Bring to a boil, reduce the heat to very low, and simmer, uncovered, stirring occasionally, until the sauce is dark and thick, about 2 hours. Let cool for 15 minutes.

Mix half of the sauce with the shredded pork. Mound the pork on a large serving platter and place the rolls on a plate. Pass the remaining sauce at the table.

1 bone-in pork shoulder, about 6 lb (3 kg)

Salt and ground pepper

1 Tbsp mustard seeds

2 cups (16 fl oz/500 ml) cider vinegar

4 yellow onions, sliced, plus 3 onions, chopped

½ cup (4 oz/125 g) unsalted butter

3 cloves garlic, chopped

2 cups (16 fl oz/500 ml) puréed canned tomatoes

2 Tbsp tomato paste

1 cup (10 oz/315 g) Peach Jam (page 42)

½ cup (4 oz/125 g) Dijon mustard (page 194 or purchased)

½ cup (4 fl oz/125 ml) aged Kentucky bourbon

½ cup (6 oz/185 g) honey

¼ cup (2 oz/60 g) firmly packed dark brown sugar

1 Tbsp hot-pepper sauce

12 soft sandwich rolls

Serves 12

Kiwifruits are often picked and eaten too green, which has given them the reputation of being flavorless. They should be soft to the touch and show some wrinkling in the skin. When eaten ripe, they are both sweet and tangy. Macerating them with sugar helps preserve their color.

Kiwi-Lemon Jam

Cut the ends off the lemon. Cut the lemon in half crosswise and remove the seeds. Place the lemon halves in a food processor, add 2 cups (1 lb/500 g) of the sugar, and process until finely puréed. Transfer to a nonreactive bowl. Cover and let stand at room temperature for at least 4 hours or up to overnight in the refrigerator.

In a nonreactive bowl, gently toss together the kiwifruit slices and the remaining 1 cup (8 oz/250 g) sugar. Cover and let stand at room temperature for 2–4 hours.

Have ready hot, sterilized jars and their lids (see page 228).

Transfer the lemon mixture to a large nonreactive saucepan. Place over medium-high heat and cook, stirring frequently, until the sugar is dissolved and the lemon becomes translucent, about 5 minutes. Add the kiwifruit mixture to the pan, reduce the heat to medium, and cook, uncovered, stirring frequently, until the jam is thick, about 5 minutes.

Ladle the hot jam into the jars, leaving ¼ inch (6 mm) of headspace. Remove any air bubbles and adjust the headspace, if necessary. Wipe the rims clean and seal tightly with the lids.

Process the jars for 10 minutes in a boiling-water bath (for detailed instructions, including cooling and testing seals, see pages 228–229). The sealed jars can be stored in a cool, dark place for up to 1 year. If a seal has failed, store the jar in the refrigerator for up to 1 month.

1 lemon, preferably Meyer

3 cups (1½ lb/750 g) sugar

3 lb (1.5 kg) kiwifruits, peeled and cut into slices ¼ inch (6 mm) thick

Makes 5 half-pint (8–fl oz/250-ml) jars

Nothing is better on an almond or peanut butter and jelly sandwich than grape jelly. You can use just about any type of grape here, although Concords or Muscats will impart the most flavor. The skins of the grapes carry most of the pectin that sets up this childhood favorite.

Grape Jelly

In a large nonreactive saucepan, combine the grapes and 1½ cups (12 fl oz/375 ml) water. Bring to a boil over medium-high heat, reduce the heat to low, and cook, uncovered, stirring frequently, until the grapes are very soft, about 15 minutes.

Suspend a jelly bag over a deep nonreactive bowl and pour the grape mixture into the bag. Let the bag stand overnight. Do not squeeze the bag, or the jelly will be cloudy.

The next day, have ready hot, sterilized jars and their lids (see page 228). Place 2 or 3 small plates in the freezer.

Remove the bag and discard the solids. Measure the grape juice, pour into a large nonreactive saucepan, and add the lemon juice. For every 1 cup (8 fl oz/250 ml) of juice, add ¾ cup (6 oz/185 g) sugar. Bring to a boil over high heat. Reduce the heat to medium-high and cook, uncovered, stirring frequently, until the jelly is thick enough to sheet off the back of a spoon, 10–15 minutes. Remove from the heat. Use 1 tsp jelly and a chilled plate to test if the jelly is ready (see page 231).

Ladle the hot jelly into the jars, leaving ¼ inch (6 mm) of headspace. Remove any air bubbles and adjust the headspace, if necessary. Wipe the rims clean and seal tightly with the lids.

Process the jars for 10 minutes in a boiling-water bath (for detailed instructions, including cooling and testing seals, see pages 228–229). The sealed jars can be stored in a cool, dark place for up to 1 year. If a seal has failed, store the jar in the refrigerator for up to 1 month.

3 lb (1.5 kg) grapes such as Concord or Muscat, stemmed and crushed

¾ cup (6 fl oz/180 ml) fresh lemon juice

About 3 cups (1½ lb/750 g) sugar, or as needed

Makes 5 half-pint (8–fl oz/250-ml) jars

If sweet Meyer lemons are in season, use them in this jelly. If you can't find them, regular lemons will do. For a variation, add lemon verbena sprigs to the jelly to give it a more savory character. Or, substitute 10 fresh thyme or rosemary sprigs for the lemon verbena.

Meyer Lemon Jelly

Cut off the stem end of each lemon. Keep the blossom end intact, as it contains pectin that will help thicken the jelly. Slice each lemon as thinly as possible, preferably on a mandoline. Place in a large nonreactive saucepan and add 3 qt (3 l) water. Bring to a boil over medium heat and cook, uncovered, stirring occasionally, for 30 minutes. Remove from the heat and let stand for about 30 minutes.

Suspend a jelly bag over a deep nonreactive bowl and pour the lemon mixture into the bag. Let the bag stand overnight. Do not squeeze the bag, or the jelly will be cloudy.

The next day, have ready hot, sterilized jars and their lids (see page 228). Place 2 or 3 small plates in the freezer.

Measure the liquid; you should have about 5 cups (40 fl oz/1.25 l). Pour the liquid into a nonreactive saucepan and add the lemon juice. Bring to a boil over medium-high heat, add the sugar, and boil rapidly, stirring frequently, until the jelly is thick enough to sheet off the back of a spoon, about 10 minutes. Remove from the heat. Use 1 tsp jelly and a chilled plate to test if the jelly is ready (see page 231).

Ladle the hot jelly into the jars, leaving ¼ inch (6 mm) of headspace. Remove any air bubbles and adjust the headspace, if necessary. Wipe the rims clean and seal tightly with the lids.

Process the jars for 10 minutes in a boiling-water bath (for detailed instructions, including cooling and testing seals, see pages 228–229). The sealed jars can be stored in a cool, dark place for up to 1 year. If a seal has failed, store the jar in the refrigerator for up to 1 month.

2 lb (1 kg) Meyer lemons

2 cups (16 fl oz/500 ml) fresh Meyer lemon juice

6 cups (3 lb/1.5 kg) sugar

Makes 7 or 8 half-pint (8–fl oz/250-ml) jars

Meyer Lemon Jelly with Lemon Verbena
Add 20 fresh lemon verbena leaves (still attached to the stems) to the lemon mixture with the sugar. Once the mixture has jelled, discard the lemon verbena.

If you don't have a stand mixer, you can still make these doughnuts: Mix the dough with a spoon until you are ready to add the ¼ cup flour. Then dust the work surface with the flour, turn the dough out onto it, and knead until smooth and springy, 8–10 minutes.

Jelly Doughnuts

In a small saucepan over medium heat, bring the milk, butter, and the 2 Tbsp sugar to a simmer. Remove from the heat and let cool to lukewarm (110°F/43°C). In a small cup, stir together the yeast and warm water and let stand until foamy, about 5 minutes.

Pour the yeast and milk mixtures into a large bowl. Lightly whisk in the eggs. Using a stand mixer with the paddle attachment, mix in 3½ cups (17½ oz/545 g) of the flour on low speed. Switch to the dough hook and beat in the remaining ¼ cup (1½ oz/45 g) flour on low speed. On medium-high speed, beat the dough until smooth and springy, about 5 minutes. Turn out onto a lightly floured work surface and knead briefly until no longer sticky. Transfer to a large buttered bowl, turn to coat, cover, and let rise until doubled in bulk, about 1½ hours.

Punch down the dough. On a lightly floured work surface, roll it out ½ inch (12 mm) thick. Using a 3-inch (7.5-cm) round biscuit cutter, cut out rounds. Put a generous tsp of jelly on half of the rounds. Top with the remaining rounds and pinch the edges, stretching and sealing them. Using the cutter, recut the rounds to seal the edges. Gather the scraps and make more doughnuts the same way. Cover with a clean kitchen towel and let stand until puffy, about 20 minutes.

Pour oil to a depth of 3 inches (7.5 cm) into a heavy-bottomed saucepan and heat to 375°F (190°C) on a deep-frying thermometer. In batches, add the doughnuts and fry, turning once, until golden brown, about 2 minutes total. Transfer to paper towels to drain briefly, then coat with the ½ cup sugar and serve warm.

1 cup (8 fl oz/250 ml) milk

2 Tbsp unsalted butter

2 Tbsp sugar plus ½ cup (4 oz/125 g) for coating

2½ tsp (1 package) active dry yeast

2 Tbsp warm water (about 110°F/43°C)

2 eggs

3¾ cups (19 oz/590 g) all-purpose (plain) flour

About ⅓ cup (3 oz/90 g) Meyer Lemon Jelly (page 51) or other jelly

Canola oil for deep frying

Makes about 12 doughnuts

You don't need to remove the mint leaves from the stems, as the latter will enhance the flavor of the jelly. Use peppermint or spearmint, or try another variety, such as orange bergamot. Although the green food coloring is optional, without it the jelly will be gold–brown.

Mint Jelly

Have ready hot, sterilized jars and their lids (see page 228). Place 2 or 3 small plates in the freezer.

Roughly chop the mint, including the stems. Place in a large nonreactive saucepan and add the pectin and vinegar. Bring to a boil over high heat and cook, stirring frequently, for 5 minutes. Stir in the sugar and return to a boil. Reduce the heat to medium and cook, uncovered, stirring frequently, until the jelly is thick enough to sheet off the back of a spoon, about 1 minute. Remove from the heat. Use 1 tsp jelly and a chilled plate to test if the jelly is ready (see page 231).

Strain the hot jelly through a fine-mesh sieve set over a bowl. Discard the mint. If desired, add drops of green food coloring.

Ladle the hot jelly into the jars, leaving ¼ inch (6 mm) of headspace. Remove any air bubbles and adjust the headspace, if necessary. Wipe the rims clean and seal tightly with the lids.

Process the jars for 10 minutes in a boiling-water bath (for detailed instructions, including cooling and testing seals, see pages 228–229). The sealed jars can be stored in a cool, dark place for up to 1 year. If a seal has failed, store the jar in the refrigerator for up to 1 month.

2 bunches fresh mint

4 cups (32 fl oz/1 l) Homemade Apple Pectin (page 231)

¼ cup (2 fl oz/60 ml) cider vinegar

4 cups (2 lb/1 kg) sugar

Green food coloring (optional)

Makes 7 or 8 half-pint (8–fl oz/250-ml) jars

The combination of lamb and mint jelly is a classic one. In this updated version, the buns for juicy lamb burgers are slathered with mint jelly and creamy yogurt sauce. Pile the burgers with pickled onions (page 156) and any other toppings, such as tomato slices, lettuce, or feta cheese.

Grilled Lamb Burgers with Mint Jelly

In a bowl, combine the lamb, onion, garlic, 2 Tbsp of the mint, the cumin, salt, and pepper. Mix well and form into 6 patties each about ½ inch (12 mm) thick. Place on a plate, cover, and refrigerate for 1 hour.

In a small bowl, mix together the yogurt, lemon juice, and remaining 1 Tbsp mint. Cover and refrigerate until ready to use.

Prepare a charcoal or gas grill for direct grilling over high heat. Clean and oil the grill rack.

Grill the lamb burgers, turning once, until medium-rare and pink when cut in the thickest portion, 4–5 minutes on each side. About halfway through grilling the burgers, place the buns, cut sides down, on the grill rack and grill until golden, about 5 minutes.

Place a grilled bun bottom on each plate and spread with the jelly and then the yogurt sauce. Top with a lamb burger and then the bun top. Serve at once, passing the remaining jelly at the table.

2 lb (1 kg) ground (minced) lamb

¼ cup (1½ oz/45 g) minced red onion

2 cloves garlic, minced

3 Tbsp chopped fresh mint

½ tsp ground cumin

1 tsp salt

½ tsp coarsely ground pepper

¾ cup (6 oz/185 g) Greek-style plain yogurt

1 Tbsp fresh lemon juice

6 hamburger buns, split

1 cup (10 oz/315 g) Mint Jelly (page 53)

Serves 6

This sweet-spicy jelly is one of the best-kept secrets of cooks in the American South. It makes a delicious glaze for pork, poultry, or lamb and is irresistible spread on bagels and corn bread or spooned over cream cheese or goat cheese on crackers or baguette slices.

Hot-Pepper Jelly

Have ready hot, sterilized jars and their lids (see page 228).

In a food processor, combine the chiles, onion, celery seeds, and ¼ cup (2 fl oz/60 ml) of the vinegar. Process until the chiles and onion are finely chopped. Transfer to a large nonreactive saucepan. Add the remaining ½ cup (4 fl oz/120 ml) vinegar and the sugar. Bring to a boil over medium-high heat and cook, uncovered, stirring frequently, for 1 minute. Remove from the heat and stir in the pectin. Return to medium-high heat and boil for 1 minute longer. Remove from the heat and let stand for 5 minutes.

Ladle the hot jelly into the jars, leaving ¼ inch (6 mm) of headspace. Remove any air bubbles and adjust the headspace, if necessary. Wipe the rims clean and seal tightly with the lids.

Process the jars for 10 minutes in a boiling-water bath (for detailed instructions, including cooling and testing seals, see pages 228–229). The sealed jars can be stored in a cool, dark place for up to 1 year. If a seal has failed, store the jar in the refrigerator for up to 1 month.

3 red jalapeño chiles, seeded and coarsely chopped

3 green jalapeño chiles, seeded and coarsely chopped

½ sweet onion such as Vidalia, chopped

1½ tsp celery seeds

¾ cup (6 fl oz/180 ml) cider vinegar

2½ cups (1¼ lb/625 g) sugar

1 cup (8 fl oz/250 ml) purchased liquid pectin

Makes 3 half-pint (8–fl oz/250-ml) jars

The jelly, which marries red and green jalapeños, lends a sweet and spicy glaze to pork loin in this remarkably simple and tasty dish. Whole fresh chiles make a colorful garnish. Sliced fennel can also be added to the pan along with the apples and onions.

Hot Pepper–Glazed Pork Loin

Preheat the oven to 400°F (200°C). Line a large baking pan with aluminum foil and lightly oil the foil.

Place the pork in the prepared pan and rub it with the salt and pepper. Roast for 15 minutes.

Reduce the oven temperature to 350°F (180°C). Spoon the jelly over the pork and spread it evenly. Pour the apple cider around the pork and scatter the apple and onion slices alongside the pork. Continue to roast the pork, basting it with the pan drippings every 10 minutes or so, until an instant-read thermometer inserted into the thickest part of the pork registers 145°F (63°C), about 45 minutes. Remove from the oven, tent loosely with aluminum foil, and let rest for 15 minutes.

Slice the pork and arrange on a warmed platter. Top with the apple and onion slices. Skim off the fat from the pan juices, then drizzle the pork with the juices. Serve at once.

1 boneless pork loin, about 4 lb (2 kg), trimmed of visible fat

1 tsp salt

1 Tbsp freshly ground pepper

1 cup (10 oz/315 g) Hot-Pepper Jelly (facing page)

⅔ cup (5 fl oz/160 ml) sweet apple cider

1 apple, preferably green or Golden Delicious, cored and thinly sliced

1 small yellow onion, thinly sliced

Serves 8

If you or a neighbor is lucky enough to have a pomegranate tree, this is a wonderful way to use the juice (see page 235). Purchased pomegranate juice can be used as well. It contains less pectin than fresh pomegranate juice, so it must be reduced further.

Pomegranate Jelly

Have ready hot, sterilized jars and their lids (see page 228). Place 2 or 3 small plates in the freezer.

In a large nonreactive saucepan over medium-high heat, bring the pomegranate juice to a boil. Add the pectin and return to a boil. Cook, uncovered, stirring frequently, until the liquid is reduced by one-third (to about 5 cups/40 fl oz/1.25 l) if using fresh pomegranate juice, and by half (to about 4 cups/32 fl oz/1 l) if using purchased pomegranate juice. Stir in the sugar, bring to a boil, and cook, stirring frequently, until the jelly is thick enough to sheet off the back of a spoon, about 1 minute. Remove from the heat. Use 1 tsp jelly and a chilled plate to test if the jelly is ready (see page 231).

Ladle the hot jelly into the jars, leaving ¼ inch (6 mm) of headspace. Remove any air bubbles and adjust the headspace, if necessary. Wipe the rims clean and seal tightly with the lids.

Process the jars for 10 minutes in a boiling-water bath (for detailed instructions, including cooling and testing seals, see pages 228–229). The sealed jars can be stored in a cool, dark place for up to 1 year. If a seal has failed, store the jar in the refrigerator for up to 1 month.

4 cups (32 fl oz/1 l) unsweetened pomegranate juice, fresh or purchased (see note)

4 cups (32 fl oz/1 l) Homemade Apple Pectin (page 231)

4 cups (2 lb/1 kg) sugar

Makes 5 half-pint (8–fl oz/250-ml) jars

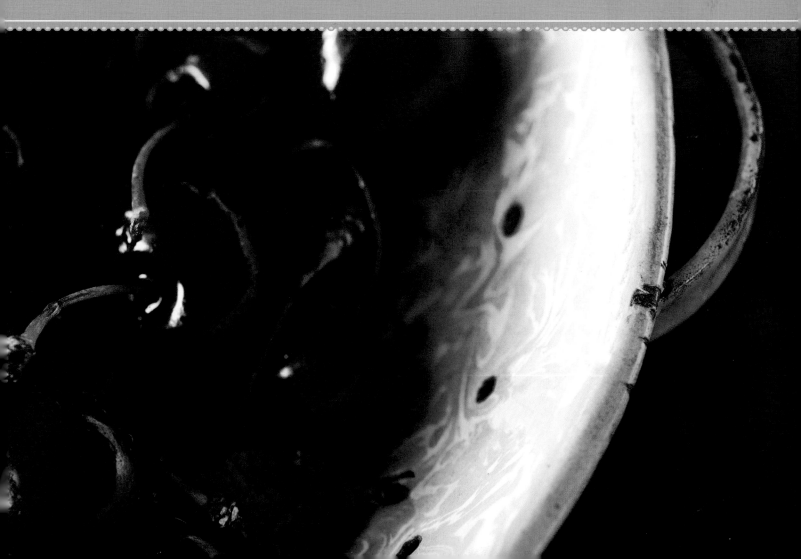

PRESERVES, CONSERVES & MARMALADES

> *"Preserving is a wonderfully creative and deeply satisfying process. It's like painting with your favorite fruits and vegetables: once you capture a vision on canvas, it becomes something entirely different."*
>
> REBECCA COURCHESNE

NECTARINES • CHERRIES • FIGS • QUINCES • LEMONS • BLOOD ORANGES

Chunkier than jams and jellies, preserves usually contain a single type of fruit, whole or sliced, suspended in a syrup or soft jelly. Conserves, a close relation, generally feature two or more fruits and typically include dried fruits and/or nuts. Whole cherries, blackberries, and figs, or sliced or halved peaches, nectarines, apricots, pears, and quinces are all good candidates for these two favorites of the preserving lexicon.

Putting up marmalades—tangy pieces of citrus peel floating in a soft, clear jelly made from the fruit's juice—is the ideal way to celebrate winter's favorite harvest. Any variety of citrus, or a mixture, can be used, from oranges and mandarins to lemons and grapefruits. Other fruits are sometimes added, as well.

Two additional hallmarks of the preserving pantry are also here: Bitter citrus peel, which is often discarded in favor of the juicy fruit it encases, is simmered in water and tossed in sugar to create a sparkly, sweet-tart candylike treat. Autumn's apples are sliced, cooked with sugar and cinnamon, and then packed into jars and stored on a shelf, ready to be poured into pie shells and baked for quick and easy desserts throughout the year.

Macerating the blackberries in sugar first produces the liquid needed for later poaching the berries. Be sure to handle the berries carefully—they are delicate and will break down easily. Serve these preserves over vanilla ice cream for a crowd-pleasing dessert.

Blackberry Preserves

In a nonreactive bowl, gently toss together the blackberries and sugar. Cover and let stand at room temperature for at least 8 hours or up to overnight in the refrigerator.

Have ready hot, sterilized jars and their lids (see page 228).

Place a sieve or colander over a large nonreactive saucepan. Pour the blackberry mixture into the sieve to drain. Remove the sieve with the berries and set aside. Bring the sugar syrup to a boil over medium heat. Add the lemon juice. The mixture will foam up; reduce the heat as necessary to prevent it from boiling over. Cook the syrup until reduced by half, 5–10 minutes. Gently stir in the blackberries and cook for 2 minutes to heat through.

Ladle the hot preserves into the jars, leaving ¼ inch (6 mm) of headspace. Remove any air bubbles and adjust the headspace, if necessary. Wipe the rims clean and seal tightly with the lids.

Process the jars for 10 minutes in a boiling-water bath (for detailed instructions, including cooling and testing seals, see pages 228–229). The sealed jars can be stored in a cool, dark place for up to 1 year. If a seal has failed, store the jar in the refrigerator for up to 1 month.

10 cups (2½ lb/1.25 kg) blackberries

3 cups (1½ lb/750 g) sugar

½ cup (4 fl oz/125 ml) fresh lemon juice

Makes 7 half-pint (8–fl oz/250-ml) jars

Ordinary cheesecake finds a perfect match when topped with juicy blackberry preserves. Even noncheesecake lovers will find these tartlets irresistible. You can use nearly any flavor of fruit preserves—cherry or blueberry would be especially delicious.

Blackberry Cheesecake Tartlets

Preheat the oven to 350°F (180°C).

To make the crust, in a food processor, combine the graham cracker crumbs, brown sugar, and melted butter. Process until the mixture starts to stick together. Remove from the food processor and firmly press the moistened crumbs onto the bottom and up the sides of eight 4½-inch (11.5-cm) tartlet pans with removable bottoms, using about ⅓ cup (1½ oz/45 g) for each pan. Bake until the crusts are set, about 8 minutes. Transfer to a wire rack and let cool, then refrigerate until cold.

Meanwhile, make the filling: In a bowl, using an electric mixer on medium speed, beat the cream cheese, granulated sugar, and vanilla until well blended. Add the cream and continue to beat on medium speed until fluffy, about 1 minute.

Place 1 Tbsp water in a small saucepan. Sprinkle the gelatin over the water and let soften for 5 minutes. Place the saucepan over low heat and stir until the gelatin dissolves. Add the gelatin mixture to the cream-cheese mixture and beat until fluffy, about 1 minute.

Spoon about ⅓ cup (3 fl oz/80 ml) of the filling into each crust and smooth the tops. Cover with aluminum foil and refrigerate for at least 2 hours or up to overnight.

Remove the pan sides from the tartlets. Spoon the preserves evenly on top of the tartlets. Refrigerate for at least 10 minutes before serving.

FOR THE CRUST

2¼ cups (7 oz/220 g) graham cracker crumbs

⅓ cup (2½ oz/75 g) firmly packed light brown sugar

½ cup (4 oz/125 g) plus 1 Tbsp unsalted butter, melted and cooled

1 lb (500 g) cream cheese, at room temperature

½ cup (4 oz/125 g) granulated sugar

1 tsp pure vanilla extract

½ cup (4 fl oz/125 ml) heavy (double) cream

½ tsp unflavored gelatin

About 1½ cups (15 oz/ 470 g) Blackberry Preserves (facing page)

Makes 8 tartlets

The lush sweetness of the figs shines through in this simple recipe. Any variety will work here. Dark-skinned figs produce an almost purple syrup; green Adriatic figs yield a pale syrup. For some spice, add a pinch of star anise. Quarter the figs and serve on crostini with goat cheese.

Fig Preserves

Have ready hot, sterilized jars and their lids (see page 228).

Trim the fig stems, leaving a little of the stem attached to each fig. In a large nonreactive saucepan, combine the sugar and orange and lemon juices. Bring to a boil over medium-high heat, stirring to dissolve the sugar. Add the figs, reduce the heat to medium, and cook, stirring gently, for 5 minutes. Using a slotted spoon, transfer the figs to a bowl. Add the orange zest to the syrup and cook, uncovered, until reduced by one-third, 2–3 minutes. Return the figs to the pan and cook for 1 minute to heat through.

Using the slotted spoon, divide the hot figs evenly among the jars. Ladle the syrup over the figs, leaving ¼ inch (6 mm) of headspace. Remove any air bubbles and adjust the headspace, if necessary. Wipe the rims clean and seal tightly with the lids.

Process the jars for 10 minutes in a boiling-water bath (for detailed instructions, including cooling and testing seals, see pages 228–229). The sealed jars can be stored in a cool, dark place for up to 1 year. If a seal has failed, store the jar in the refrigerator for up to 1 month.

3 lb (1.5 kg) figs such as Mission, Adriatic, or Brown Turkey

4 cups (2 lb/1 kg) sugar

1¼ cups (10 fl oz/310 ml) fresh orange juice

¾ cup (6 fl oz/180 ml) fresh lemon juice

Grated zest of 1 orange

Makes 5 half-pint (8-fl oz/250-ml) jars

Ordinary grilled cheese sandwiches become special when you use an out-of-the-ordinary filling. Salty prosciutto, smooth fontina, and gooey fig preserves combine to create a memorably delicious sandwich. Mozzarella cheese can be substituted for the fontina.

Prosciutto Panini with Fontina & Fig Preserves

Place 4 of the bread slices on a work surface. Divide the cheese among the bread slices, and then top the cheese with even amounts of fig preserves and prosciutto slices. Cover with the remaining bread slices.

Place a large, heavy frying pan over medium-high heat. Pour in enough oil to evenly coat the bottom. When the pan is hot, working in batches, add the sandwiches to the pan and cook, pressing down often with a metal spatula, until golden brown on the undersides, 2–3 minutes. Turn the sandwiches, adding more oil to the pan if necessary to prevent scorching. Cook, again pressing down on the sandwiches, until golden brown on the second sides, about 2 minutes longer.

Cut the sandwiches on the diagonal and serve at once.

8 large slices coarse country bread, each about ½ inch (12 mm) thick

5–6 oz (155–185 g) fontina cheese, sliced

½ cup (5 oz/155 g) Fig Preserves (page 66), drained and sliced

8 thin slices prosciutto, about ¼ lb (125 g) total weight

About 3 Tbsp olive oil

Makes 4 sandwiches

These bright, tangy preserves have a subtle but alluring hint of earthy cardamom. Spoon the apricots over pound cake and add a dollop of whipped cream. Or, pair the preserves with cheese—fresh goat cheese or a hard cheese like Manchego both work well.

Apricot-Orange Preserves

Have ready hot, sterilized jars and their lids (see page 228).

Using a vegetable peeler, remove the zest from 1 orange in strips about 1 inch (2.5 cm) wide. Remove as much pith as possible from the strips and then cut them crosswise into very thin strips. Squeeze enough juice from the orange(s) to measure ¾ cup (6 fl oz/180 ml).

In a large nonreactive saucepan, combine the orange juice, sugar, and ¼ cup (2 fl oz/60 ml) water. Bring to a boil over medium heat. The mixture will foam up; reduce the heat as necessary to prevent it from boiling over. Stir in the apricots, lemon juice, cardamom pods, ground cardamom, and vanilla bean. Bring to a boil over medium-high heat, then reduce the heat to medium and simmer, stirring occasionally and being careful not to break up the apricots, for 5–10 minutes longer. Stir in the orange zest. Continue to cook, stirring occasionally, until the apricots are softened but still retain their shape, 5–10 minutes. Using a slotted spoon, transfer the apricots to a bowl. Cook the syrup until reduced by one-third, about 3 minutes. Return the apricots to the pan and cook over medium-low heat for 2 minutes to heat through.

Ladle the hot apricots into the jars, leaving ¼ inch (6 mm) of headspace. Remove any air bubbles and adjust the headspace, if necessary. Wipe the rims clean and seal tightly with the lids.

Process the jars for 10 minutes in a boiling-water bath (for detailed instructions, including cooling and testing seals, see pages 228–229). The sealed jars can be stored in a cool, dark place for up to 1 year. If a seal has failed, store the jar in the refrigerator for up to 1 month.

---

1 or 2 oranges

3 cups (1½ lb/750 g) sugar

3–3½ lb (1.5–1.75 kg) apricots, pitted and halved, or quartered if large (about 12 cups)

½ cup (4 fl oz/125 ml) fresh lemon juice

2 or 3 whole cardamom pods

⅛ tsp ground cardamom

¼ vanilla bean, halved

Makes 7 half-pint (8–fl oz/250-ml) jars

Toast with butter and jam takes on a new and decadent form in this rich, custardlike bread pudding. The key to the success of this pudding is the bread itself. Use a good Italian or French type with a fairly tough crumb that will hold up in liquid, without getting mushy.

Apricot-Orange Bread Pudding

Preheat the oven to 325°F (165°C). Butter a shallow 2-qt (2-l) baking dish. Have ready a large baking pan about 3 inches (7.5 cm) deep.

Spread the bread slices evenly with the butter and preserves. Cut the slices into large chunks and spread the chunks out in the prepared dish, layering them as necessary. Set the dish aside.

In a saucepan over medium heat, warm the milk and cream until small bubbles appear along the edge of the pan. Remove from the heat. In a large bowl, whisk together the sugar, whole eggs, and egg yolks. Gradually whisk in the hot milk mixture until blended.

Place the baking dish in the baking pan. Pour enough of the milk mixture into the baking dish to reach halfway up the bottom layer of bread; let stand for a few minutes until partially absorbed. Pour in the remaining milk mixture. Using a spatula, press down on the bread for a few seconds so it absorbs more liquid. Pour the boiling water into the baking pan to reach halfway up the sides of the dish.

Bake until the custard is just set and a knife inserted near the center comes out clean, 40–45 minutes. Let cool slightly on a wire rack.

6–8 slices Italian or French bread, each ½ inch (12 mm) thick

2–3 Tbsp unsalted butter, at room temperature

About ½ cup (5 oz/155 g) Apricot-Orange Preserves (page 69)

3 cups (24 fl oz/750 ml) milk

1 cup (8 fl oz/250 ml) heavy (double) cream

½ cup (4 oz/125 g) granulated sugar

3 whole eggs plus 4 egg yolks

Boiling water

Serves 6–8

Serve these elegant, bright orange kumquats whole or sliced alongside cake or over ice cream. The syrup can be added to sparkling water for a refreshing spritzer. Boiling the kumquats first removes any bitterness and helps the fruits cook more quickly in the sugar syrup.

Kumquat Preserves

Have ready hot, sterilized jars and their lids (see page 228).

In a large nonreactive saucepan, combine the kumquats with water to cover. The amount of water may be difficult to judge, as the kumquats will float. Bring to a boil over high heat. Reduce the heat to medium and cook, uncovered, for 10 minutes. Drain the kumquats.

In the same pan over high heat, combine the sugar and 4 cups (32 fl oz/1 l) water and bring to a boil, stirring to dissolve the sugar. Add the kumquats and return to a boil. Reduce the heat to low and cook, uncovered, until the kumquats are translucent and can be pierced with a knife, about 1 hour. Cover and let stand at room temperature for 8 hours or up to overnight.

Using a slotted spoon, transfer the kumquats to a bowl. Add the lemon juice to the syrup and cook, uncovered, over medium-high heat until reduced by one-third, 5–10 minutes. Add the kumquats, reduce the heat to low, and simmer for 2 minutes to heat through.

Using the slotted spoon, divide the hot kumquats evenly among the jars. Ladle the syrup over the kumquats, leaving ¼ inch (6 mm) of headspace. Remove any air bubbles and adjust the headspace, if necessary. Wipe the rims clean and seal tightly with the lids.

Process the jars for 10 minutes in a boiling-water bath (for detailed instructions, including cooling and testing seals, see pages 228–229). The sealed jars can be stored in a cool, dark place for up to 1 year. If a seal has failed, store the jar in the refrigerator for up to 1 month.

2 lb (1 kg) kumquats, stems removed

2½ cups (20 oz/625 g) sugar

½ cup (4 fl oz/125 ml) fresh lemon juice

Makes 4 half-pint (8–fl oz/250-ml) jars

Quinces, which are downy, lumpy applelike fruits, must be cooked before eating. Their sweet, slightly floral flavor and high pectin content make them perfect for preserving. Serve these preserves as they do in Spain: on bread or crackers with slices of Manchego cheese.

Quince Preserves

Have ready hot, sterilized jars and their lids (see page 228).

Place the quince peels, cores, and seeds on a square of cheesecloth (muslin), bring the corners together, and tie securely with kitchen string. Slice the quinces and place in a nonreactive saucepan. Add water to cover and the cloth bag and bring to a boil over medium-high heat. Reduce the heat to low and cook, uncovered, stirring occasionally, until very tender, 20–40 minutes, adding more water if needed to keep covered.

Discard the cloth bag. Stir in 3½ cups of the sugar, bring to a simmer over low heat, and cook, uncovered, stirring often, until the preserves are thick, about 20 minutes. Taste and adjust with more sugar if too tart.

Ladle the hot preserves into the jars, leaving ¼ inch (6 mm) of headspace. Remove any air bubbles and adjust the headspace, if necessary. Wipe the rims clean and seal tightly with the lids.

Process the jars for 10 minutes in a boiling-water bath (for detailed instructions, including cooling and testing seals, see pages 228–229). The sealed jars can be stored in a cool, dark place for up to 1 year. If a seal has failed, store the jar in the refrigerator for up to 1 month.

2 lb (1 kg) quinces, peeled, halved, and cored, with peels, cores, and seeds reserved

3½–4 cups (1¾–2 lb/ 875 g–1 kg) sugar

Makes 4 half-pint (8–fl oz/250-ml) jars

Make sure that each serving of this delectable flatbread includes a bit of everything—mildly floral preserves, Gorgonzola cheese, pine nuts, and peppery arugula—for the ultimate sweet and savory bite. If desired, top with a light drizzle of extra-virgin olive oil just before serving.

Flatbread with Quince Preserves & Gorgonzola

To make the dough, in a small bowl, sprinkle the yeast over the ¾ cup warm water and let stand until foamy, about 5 minutes. Stir in the olive oil and salt. In a food processor, combine the flour and the yeast mixture. Process until a soft dough forms, about 45 seconds, adding more water or flour if necessary. Turn out the dough onto a lightly floured work surface and knead until smooth and springy, 5–8 minutes. Transfer to a lightly oiled bowl, cover with plastic wrap, and let rise in a warm place until doubled in volume, about 1 hour.

Divide the dough in half. Cover the dough with a clean kitchen towel and let stand for 10 minutes.

Preheat the oven to 450°F (230°C). Lightly oil 2 rimmed baking sheets and sprinkle with cornmeal. Roll or stretch each portion of dough into a 13-by-7-inch (33-by-18-cm) oval about ⅛ inch (3 mm) thick and place on a prepared baking sheet. Prick the dough evenly with a fork and brush lightly with olive oil.

Bake until the flatbreads are crisp and golden, 10–12 minutes. Evenly brush each flatbread with the preserves, and then top with the cheese, pine nuts, and arugula. Break the flatbreads into large pieces or cut into wedges and serve at once.

FOR THE DOUGH

1 tsp active dry yeast

¾ cup (6 fl oz/180 ml) warm water (110°F/43°C), plus extra if needed

2 Tbsp olive oil, plus more for brushing

½ tsp salt

2 cups (10 oz/315 g) all-purpose (plain) flour, plus extra if needed

Cornmeal for sprinkling

⅓ cup (4 oz/125 g) Quince Preserves (page 73)

¼ lb (125 g) Gorgonzola cheese, sliced or crumbled

¼ cup (1 oz/30 g) pine nuts, toasted

2 cups (2 oz/60 g) baby arugula (rocket)

Makes two 13-by-7-inch (33-by-18-cm) flatbreads

Apple Pie Filling

Making pie fillings to enjoy months later is a great solution to putting up bumper crops of fruit, and also makes for an always-welcome gift. For Blueberry Pie Filling, see page 232.

9½ lb (4.75 kg) apples	¾ cup (3 oz/90 g) ClearJel starch (see note on facing page)
¾ cup (6 fl oz/180 ml) bottled lemon juice	1½ tsp ground cinnamon
2½ cups (1¼ lb/625 g) sugar, or as needed	2½ cups (20 fl oz/625 ml) apple juice

Have ready hot, clean jars and their lids (see page 228). Bring a large pot of water to a boil. Meanwhile, pour ¼ cup (2 fl oz/60 ml) of the lemon juice into a large bowl. Peel, core, and slice the apples, dropping the slices into the bowl. Toss the slices with the lemon juice to prevent browning. Add the slices to the boiling water and blanch for 1 minute. Drain the slices, return to the pot, and cover to keep warm.

In a large nonreactive saucepan, stir together the sugar, ClearJel starch, cinnamon, and apple juice. Add 1¼ cups (10 fl oz/310 ml) water. Bring to a boil over medium-high heat, stirring frequently. Reduce the heat to medium-low and simmer, stirring constantly, until translucent and slightly thickened, 1–2 minutes. Stir in the remaining ½ cup (4 fl oz/125 ml) lemon juice. Fold in the apples and stir until warm, if necessary.

Ladle the hot apple mixture into the jars, leaving 1 inch (2.5 cm) of headspace. Remove any air bubbles and adjust the headspace, if necessary. Wipe the rims clean and seal tightly with the lids.

Process the jars for 25 minutes in a boiling-water bath (for detailed instructions, including cooling and testing seals, see pages 228–229). The sealed jars can be stored in a cool, dark place for up to 1 year. If a seal has failed, store the jar in the refrigerator for up to 1 week.

Makes 7 one-pint (16–fl oz/500-ml) jars

Pies by the pint

This pie-filling recipe yields just enough to fill a canner—7 one-pint (16–fl oz/500-ml) jars. If your canner can hold one-quart (1-l) jars, simply double the recipe to make 7 quart-size jars. One quart-size jar, or 2 pint-size ones, provides just the right amount of filling for a 9-inch (23-cm) pie shell.

How to bake

Once poured into a pie shell, this pie filling will cook in about two-thirds the time it takes to cook raw apples in a pie. Pour it into a pie shell, top with a plain or lattice crust, and bake in a preheated 350°F (180°C) oven until the crust is golden, about 40 minutes. For a simple pie dough recipe, see page 232.

The best thickener

For canning recipes that would otherwise require cornstarch, such as pie fillings, the USDA recommends using ClearJel starch. Unlike ordinary cornstarch, ClearJel does not break down when combined with acidic ingredients and tolerates the high temperatures needed for successful canning. ClearJel can be ordered online from baking supply companies.

Blueberry season is too short. Before you know it, they're gone, which is all the more reason to make these preserves. Although you can find them in grocery stores, the freshest blueberries typically come from farmers' markets. Here, the citrus brightens their flavor.

Blueberry-Citrus Preserves

Have ready hot, sterilized jars and their lids (see page 228).

Using a vegetable peeler, remove the zest from one of the oranges in strips about 1 inch (2.5 cm) wide. Remove as much pith as possible from the strips and then cut them crosswise into thin strips. Cut both oranges in half and squeeze enough juice to measure 1 cup (8 fl oz/250 ml).

In a large nonreactive saucepan over medium heat, combine the sugar and orange juice. Bring to a simmer and cook, stirring frequently, until the sugar is dissolved and the syrup is bubbling. Add the blueberries, lemon juice, and zest strips. Bring to a boil over medium-high heat, reduce the heat to medium, and cook, uncovered, stirring occasionally, for 5–8 minutes. The mixture should consist of whole berries floating in a dark, thick syrup.

Using a slotted spoon, divide the hot berries among the jars. Ladle the syrup over the berries, covering them completely and leaving ¼ inch (6 mm) of headspace. Remove any air bubbles and adjust the headspace, if necessary. Wipe the rims clean and seal tightly with the lids.

Process the jars for 10 minutes in a boiling-water bath (for detailed instructions, including cooling and testing seals, see pages 228–229). The sealed jars can be stored in a cool, dark place for up to 1 year. If a seal has failed, store the jar in the refrigerator for up to 1 month.

2 oranges

2 cups (1 lb/500 g) sugar

8 cups (2 lb/1 kg) blueberries, stems removed

½ cup (4 fl oz/125 ml) fresh lemon juice

Makes 5 half-pint (8–fl oz/250-ml) jars

Enjoy moist and flavorful blueberry muffins year-round by using blueberry preserves instead of fresh berries. If your preserves are syrupy, drain them before adding them to the batter to ensure that the muffins aren't too sweet and that the syrup doesn't turn the batter purple.

Blueberry-Citrus Muffins

Preheat the oven to 400°F (200°C). Grease 16 standard muffin cups; fill any unused cups with water to prevent warping.

In a large bowl, stir together the flour, baking powder, baking soda, and salt. In another bowl, whisk together the sugar, milk, sour cream, oil, egg, and orange zest until well combined. Add to the flour mixture and stir just until blended.

Place a spoonful of batter into each prepared muffin cup. Top with a generous Tbsp of the preserves, and then spoon the remaining batter on top, filling each cup about two-thirds full.

Bake until a toothpick inserted into the center of a muffin comes out clean, 15–18 minutes. Let cool in the muffin pans on a wire rack for 3–5 minutes. Unmold the muffins and serve warm.

2¼ cups (11½ oz/360 g) all-purpose (plain) flour

2 tsp baking powder

1 tsp baking soda (bicarbonate of soda)

½ tsp salt

¾ cup (6 oz/185 g) sugar

½ cup (4 fl oz/125 ml) milk

½ cup (4 fl oz/125 ml) sour cream

⅓ cup (3 fl oz/80 ml) canola oil

1 egg

1 Tbsp grated orange zest

About 1 cup (10 oz/315 g) Blueberry-Citrus Preserves (opposite page), strained if necessary

Makes 16 muffins

Keeping the pits in the cherries gives the preserves a subtle almond flavor, and eliminates an arduous task. Just remember to warn diners about the pits before they savor the preserve (or, if you prefer, pit the cherries). Spoon the preserves over ice cream for a winter dessert.

Cherry Preserves

Have ready hot, sterilized jars and their lids (see page 228).

In a large nonreactive saucepan, combine the sugar and lemon juice. Add 2 cups (16 fl oz/500 ml) water and bring to a boil over medium-high heat, stirring to dissolve the sugar. Add the cherries, reduce the heat to medium, and cook, stirring gently, for 5 minutes. Using a slotted spoon, transfer the cherries to a rimmed baking sheet or a large platter, spreading them out in an even layer. Cook the syrup until reduced by half, about 5 minutes. Return the cherries to the pan and cook for 1 minute to heat through.

Using the slotted spoon, divide the hot cherries evenly among the jars. Ladle the syrup over the cherries, leaving ¼ inch (6 mm) of headspace. Remove any air bubbles and adjust the headspace, if necessary. Wipe the rims clean and seal tightly with the lids.

Process the jars for 10 minutes in a boiling-water bath (for detailed instructions, including cooling and testing seals, see pages 228–229). The sealed jars can be stored in a cool, dark place for up to 1 year. If a seal has failed, store the jar in the refrigerator for up to 1 month.

4 cups (2 lb/1 kg) sugar

¼ cup (2 fl oz/60 ml) fresh lemon juice

2½ lb (1.25 kg) dark sweet cherries such as Bing (about 8 cups), stems removed

Makes 5 half-pint (8–fl oz/250-ml) jars

Cherries Preserved in Wine
Substitute 1 cup (8 fl oz/ 250 ml) *each* water and fruity red wine, such as Zinfandel or Cabernet Franc, for the 2 cups water and ¼ cup lemon juice.

A sweet cherry sauce accents roasted duck breasts for an elegant meal that is surprisingly simple to prepare. A Pinot Noir, with its cherry undertones, would be a nice accompaniment. Be sure to remove the cherry pits, if necessary, before adding the preserves to the sauce.

Pan-Roasted Duck Breasts with Cherry Sauce

Preheat the oven to 375°F (190°C).

Season the duck breasts on both sides with salt and pepper. Heat a large ovenproof frying pan over high heat until hot. Add the olive oil and swirl to coat the pan. When the oil is hot, add the duck breasts, skinned side down. Reduce the heat to medium-high and cook until browned on the first side, 1½–2 minutes. Turn and cook until the second side is lightly browned, another 1½–2 minutes. Transfer the pan to the oven and roast until an instant-read thermometer inserted into the thickest part of a breast registers 125°F (52°C), about 5 minutes for medium-rare. Transfer the breasts to a platter, tent loosely with aluminum foil, and let rest while you make the sauce.

Pour off any fat in the frying pan. Place over medium-low heat and add 1 Tbsp of the butter. When the butter is melted, add the shallot and sauté until softened, about 2 minutes. Add the Port and dried cherries, raise the heat to high, and simmer until the pan is almost dry. Add the reduced broth, preserves, vinegar, and any accumulated juices on the platter. Boil until the sauce is reduced to about ⅔ cup (5 fl oz/160 ml) and is almost syrupy. Remove from the heat and add the remaining 3 Tbsp butter. Swirl the pan until the butter melts.

Slice the duck breasts on the diagonal and transfer to warmed individual plates. Top with the sauce, dividing it evenly, and serve at once.

4 boneless, skinless duck breast halves

Salt and freshly ground pepper

1 Tbsp olive oil

4 Tbsp (2 oz/60 g) unsalted butter

1 large shallot, minced

¾ cup (6 fl oz/180 ml) Port

⅓ cup (2 oz/60 g) dried pitted sweet cherries

2 cups (16 fl oz/500 ml) chicken broth, boiled until reduced by half

4 Tbsp (2½ oz/75 g) Cherry Preserves (page 81)

2 tsp balsamic vinegar

Serves 4

For a fantastic variation on this classic favorite, add fresh basil, which brings a bright herbal note to these sweet, summery preserves. Either version makes an excellent accompaniment to grilled meat, especially chicken or pork, or a sweet addition to a savory cheese plate.

Nectarine Preserves

In a deep nonreactive dish, gently toss together the nectarines and sugar. Cover and refrigerate for at least 8 hours or up to overnight.

Have ready hot, sterilized jars and their lids (see page 228).

Place a colander over a large nonreactive saucepan. Pour the nectarine and sugar mixture into the colander to drain. Remove the colander with the nectarines and set aside. Bring the sugar syrup to a boil over medium heat. The mixture will foam up; reduce the heat as necessary to prevent it from boiling over. Add the nectarines and lemon juice, raise the heat to medium-high, and cook, stirring occasionally and being careful not to break up the nectarines, until the nectarines are softened but still retain their shape, about 10 minutes.

Using a slotted spoon, divide the hot nectarines evenly among the jars. Ladle the syrup over the nectarines, leaving ¼ inch (6 mm) of headspace. Remove any air bubbles and adjust the headspace, if necessary. Wipe the rims clean and seal tightly with the lids.

Process the jars for 10 minutes in a boiling-water bath (for detailed instructions, including cooling and testing seals, see pages 228–229). The sealed jars can be stored in a cool, dark place for up to 1 year. If a seal has failed, store the jar in the refrigerator for up to 1 month.

2–2½ lb (1–1.25 kg) nectarines, pitted and sliced (about 10 cups)

2 cups (1 lb/500 g) sugar

½ cup (4 fl oz/125 ml) fresh lemon juice

Makes 5 half-pint (8–fl oz/250-ml) jars

Nectarine-Basil Preserves
Rinse and dry 6 fresh basil sprigs. Toss the basil with the nectarines and sugar, making sure the sprigs are evenly distributed. Refrigerate as directed. Remove the basil after pouring the fruit mixture into the colander.

Blood oranges are in season only briefly, so make this recipe before they are gone. Their sweet–tart juice and slightly bitter peel are ideal for marmalade. Use a mandoline, if possible, to slice the oranges thinly. Do not overcook the marmalade or it will have a caramel flavor.

Blood Orange Marmalade

Have ready hot, sterilized jars and their lids (see page 228). Place 2 or 3 small plates in the freezer.

Cut off the stem ends of the oranges. Slice each orange as thinly as possible, preferably on a mandoline. Place in a large nonreactive saucepan and add 8 cups (64 fl oz/2 l) water. Bring to a boil over medium-high heat and cook, uncovered, stirring frequently, for 15 minutes. Remove from the heat and let cool slightly.

Measure the orange slices and their liquid and return to the pan. For each 1 cup (8 fl oz/250 ml), add ¾ cup (6 oz/185 g) sugar. Stir in the orange and lemon juices. Bring to a boil over medium-high heat and boil rapidly for 10 minutes. Reduce the heat to medium and cook, stirring frequently, until slightly thickened and gelatinous, 7–10 minutes longer. Remove from the heat. Use 1 tsp marmalade and a chilled plate to test if the marmalade is ready (see page 231).

Ladle the hot marmalade into the jars, leaving ¼ inch (6 mm) of headspace. Remove any air bubbles and adjust the headspace, if necessary. Wipe the rims clean and seal tightly with the lids.

Process the jars for 10 minutes in a boiling-water bath (for detailed instructions, including cooling and testing seals, see pages 228–229). The sealed jars can be stored in a cool, dark place for up to 1 year. If a seal has failed, store the jar in the refrigerator for up to 1 month.

2 lb (1 kg) blood oranges

About 6 cups (3 lb/1.5 kg) sugar, or as needed

2 cups (16 fl oz/500 ml) fresh blood orange juice

½ cup (4 fl oz/125 ml) fresh lemon juice

Makes 7 half-pint (8–fl oz/250-ml) jars

Chicken thighs are perfect for roasting, resulting in moist and flavorful meat. Adding the marmalade glaze at the end of roasting keeps the skin crispy and savory, and also turns it a shiny gold–orange. Any type of orange marmalade can be used here.

Chicken Thighs with Blood Orange Glaze

Preheat the oven to 425°F (220°C). Lightly oil a roasting pan large enough to accommodate the thighs in a single layer without crowding.

In a small bowl, stir together the cumin, salt, and pepper. Brush the chicken thighs on all sides with the olive oil, and then season on all sides with the cumin mixture. Press the mixture firmly into the skin so that it sticks. Arrange the thighs, skin side up, in the prepared pan. Roast until the skin is lightly golden, about 20 minutes.

Meanwhile, make the glaze: In a small saucepan over medium heat, melt the butter. Add the shallot and cook, stirring, until softened, about 2 minutes. Stir in the marmalade, vinegar, mustard, and pepper and cook, stirring, until the marmalade melts. Give the cornstarch mixture a quick stir, add to the pan, and cook, stirring, just until the glaze is thickened, about 30 seconds.

Brush the skin side of the chicken thighs generously with the glaze and continue to roast for 5 minutes. Brush the thighs again with the glaze, return them to the oven, and roast until an instant-read thermometer inserted into the thickest part of a thigh away from the bone registers 165°–170°F (74°–77°C), 5–10 minutes longer. Transfer the chicken to a platter and serve at once.

1 tsp ground cumin

1½ tsp salt

½ tsp freshly ground pepper

8 skin-on, bone-in chicken thighs (about 3 lb/1.5 kg total weight)

2 Tbsp olive oil

FOR THE GLAZE

1 Tbsp unsalted butter

1 shallot, minced

1 cup (10 oz/315 g) Blood Orange Marmalade (page 84)

¼ cup (2 fl oz/60 ml) cider vinegar

1 Tbsp Dijon mustard (page 194 or purchased)

1 tsp freshly ground pepper

1 tsp cornstarch (cornflour) mixed with 1 Tbsp cold water

Serves 4

French crêpes, which are popular around the world, are easy to make once you master swirling the pan to coat it thinly and evenly with the batter. Filled with bright and sweet marmalade, they will be a hit at breakfast or for dessert.

Crêpes with Meyer Lemon–Ginger Marmalade

In a blender, combine the flour, sugar, 1½ cups milk, eggs, melted butter, and vanilla. Process until well blended. Pour into a measuring pitcher with a spout, cover, and refrigerate for 2–4 hours. If the batter seems thick and sluggish, thin with a bit of milk or water to the consistency of heavy (double) cream.

Line a plate with waxed paper. Place an 8- or 9-inch (20- or 23-cm) nonstick frying pan over medium heat and melt just enough of the remaining 2 Tbsp butter to coat it lightly. When hot, pour in 2–3 Tbsp of the batter and tilt the pan, swirling the batter until the bottom is evenly covered. Pour any excess batter back into the pitcher. Cook until bubbles appear on the surface, about 1 minute. Turn the crêpe and cook on the second side until just set, 10–20 seconds longer. Turn out onto the lined plate. Cook the remaining batter in the same way, adding butter as needed and placing waxed paper between the crêpes. You should have 12 crêpes.

Spread each crêpe evenly with about 2 tsp marmalade. Fold the crêpe over once and then again so that it is folded into quarters.

In a large nonstick frying pan over medium heat, melt 1 tsp of the remaining butter. Add 4 filled crêpes and cook, turning once, until browned on both sides, 1–1½ minutes per side. Transfer to a warmed platter. Repeat with the remaining butter and crêpes.

Arrange 2 or 3 crêpes each on warmed individual plates. Sprinkle with the lemon zest and dust with the confectioners' sugar. Serve at once.

1 cup (5 oz/155 g) all-purpose (plain) flour

1 Tbsp granulated sugar

1½ cups (12 fl oz/375 ml) milk, plus extra if needed

3 eggs

2 Tbsp unsalted butter, melted and cooled slightly, plus about 2 Tbsp unmelted

1 tsp pure vanilla extract

½ cup (5 oz/155 g) Meyer Lemon–Ginger Marmalade (page 89) or other fruit preserves

1 Tbsp grated lemon zest

Confectioners' (icing) sugar for dusting

Serves 4–6

For the best texture, the lemons must be sliced very thinly, which is most easily done with a mandoline. The liberal use of lemon juice brings out the floral qualities of the Meyer lemon, which are tempered in cooking. The ginger (fresh and crystallized) can be omitted if desired.

Meyer Lemon–Ginger Marmalade

Have ready hot, sterilized jars and their lids (see page 228). Place 2 or 3 small plates in the freezer.

Cut off the ends of each lemon. Slice each lemon as thinly as possible, preferably on a mandoline. Place the slices in a large nonreactive saucepan and add 8 cups (64 fl oz/2 l) water. Bring to a boil over medium-high heat and cook, uncovered, stirring occasionally, for 15 minutes. Remove from the heat.

Measure the lemon slices and their liquid and return to the saucepan. For each 1 cup (8 fl oz/250 ml), add 1¼ cups (10 oz/315 g) sugar. Add the lemon juice. Bring to a boil over medium heat and boil rapidly, stirring occasionally, for 10 minutes. Add the fresh ginger and continue to boil, stirring occasionally, until slightly thickened, 10–15 minutes longer. Remove from the heat. Use 1 tsp marmalade and a chilled plate to test if the marmalade is ready (see page 231). When the marmalade is ready, stir in the crystallized ginger.

Ladle the hot marmalade into the jars, leaving ¼ inch (6 mm) of headspace. Remove any air bubbles and adjust the headspace, if necessary. Wipe the rims clean and seal tightly with the lids.

Process the jars for 10 minutes in a boiling-water bath (for detailed instructions, including cooling and testing seals, see pages 228–229). The sealed jars can be stored in a cool, dark place for up to 1 year. If a seal has failed, store the jar in the refrigerator for up to 1 month.

2 lb (1 kg) Meyer lemons

About 8 cups (4 lb/2 kg) sugar, or as needed

2 cups (16 fl oz/500 ml) fresh Meyer lemon juice

1 Tbsp peeled and grated fresh ginger

1 Tbsp finely chopped crystallized ginger

Makes 7 or 8 half-pint (8–fl oz/250-ml) jars

Satsumas are usually the first mandarin oranges available in the autumn, making this marmalade an ideal choice to prepare for the holidays. If the satsumas are too tart, add more sugar (but don't decrease the amount of sugar, or the marmalade may not set).

Satsuma Marmalade

Have ready hot, sterilized jars and their lids (see page 228). Place 2 or 3 small plates in the freezer.

Halve the satsumas and extract, strain, and refrigerate the juice. Place the peels in a large nonreactive saucepan, add 8 cups (64 fl oz/2 l) water, and bring to a boil over medium-high heat. Reduce the heat to low and cook, uncovered, until the peels can be pierced with a knife, about 40 minutes. Remove from the heat. Using a slotted spoon, set the peels aside; reserve the cooking liquid. Scoop the membranes and pith from the peels and reserve. Cut the peels into long strips ⅛ inch (3 mm) wide.

Add the peels, satsuma juice, sugar, and lemon juice to the saucepan with the cooking liquid. Place the membranes and pith on a square of cheesecloth (muslin), bring the corners together, and tie securely with kitchen string. Add to the pan. Bring to a boil over medium-high heat, reduce the heat to medium, and cook, uncovered, stirring frequently, for 30 minutes. Remove from the heat. Use 1 tsp marmalade and a chilled plate to test if the marmalade is ready (see page 231).

Ladle the hot marmalade into the jars, leaving ¼ inch (6 mm) of headspace. Remove any air bubbles and adjust the headspace, if necessary. Wipe the rims clean and seal tightly with the lids.

Process the jars for 10 minutes in a boiling-water bath (for detailed instructions, including cooling and testing seals, see pages 228–229). The sealed jars can be stored in a cool, dark place for up to 1 year. If a seal has failed, store the jar in the refrigerator for up to 1 month.

5 lb (2.5 kg) satsuma mandarins

3 cups (1½ lb/750 g) sugar

½ cup (4 fl oz/125 ml) fresh lemon juice

Makes 4 half-pint (8–fl oz/250-ml) jars

Grapefruit makes a wonderful marmalade, as the peel, though thick, turns beautifully translucent when cooked. You can make the marmalade with any combination of grapefruit varieties. Serve this delicious spread on thick slices of toast at breakfast.

Ruby Grapefruit Marmalade

Have ready hot, sterilized jars and their lids (see page 228). Place 2 or 3 small plates in the freezer.

Halve the grapefruits and extract, strain, and refrigerate the juice. Place the peels in a large nonreactive saucepan, add 3 qt (3 l) water, and bring to a boil over medium-high heat. Reduce the heat to low and cook, uncovered, until the peels can be easily pierced with a knife, about 45 minutes. Remove from the heat. Using a slotted spoon, set the peels aside; reserve 4 cups (32 fl oz/1 l) of the cooking liquid. Scoop the membranes and pith from the peels and reserve. Cut the peels into long strips ⅛ inch (3 mm) wide.

In the same saucepan, combine the peels, grapefruit juice, sugar, lemon juice, and cooking liquid. Place the membranes and pith on a square of cheesecloth (muslin), bring the corners together, and tie securely with kitchen string. Add to the pan. Bring to a boil over medium-high heat, reduce the heat to medium, and cook, uncovered, stirring frequently, for 40 minutes. Remove from the heat. Use 1 tsp marmalade and a chilled plate to test if the marmalade is ready (see page 231).

Ladle the hot marmalade into the jars, leaving ¼ inch (6 mm) of headspace. Remove any air bubbles and adjust the headspace, if necessary. Wipe the rims clean and seal tightly with the lids.

Process the jars for 10 minutes in a boiling-water bath (for detailed instructions, including cooling and testing seals, see pages 228–229). The sealed jars can be stored in a cool, dark place for up to 1 year. If a seal has failed, store the jar in the refrigerator for up to 1 month.

6 lb (3 kg) ruby grapefruits

5 cups (2½ lb/1.25 kg) sugar

½ cup (4 fl oz/125 ml) fresh lemon juice

Makes 9 half-pint (8–fl oz/250-ml) jars

Candied Citrus Peel

Strips of succulent citrus peel are candied in syrup, then rolled in superfine sugar. Sweet and tangy, they make a perfect gift. Use any type of citrus peel you like or use a mix as below.

2 oranges, blood oranges, or tangerines

1 lemon

1 grapefruit

3½ cups (1½ lb/750 g) superfine (caster) sugar

Scrub the fruit thoroughly under cold running water to remove any dirt and wax. Working with 1 piece of fruit at a time, cut a thin slice from the blossom and stem ends. Working from the top to the bottom, score through the outer peel and white pith to the flesh, spacing the cuts about 1 inch (2.5 cm) apart. Peel the fruit. Cut each peel section lengthwise into long strips about ¼ inch (6 mm) wide. (Reserve the flesh for another use.)

In a large nonreactive saucepan, combine the peels with water to cover by 2 inches (5 cm). Bring to a boil, reduce the heat to low, and simmer, uncovered, until the peels begin to soften, 40–45 minutes. Drain.

In the same saucepan over medium-high heat, combine 1½ cups (10 oz/310 g) of the sugar and 2 cups (16 fl oz/500 ml) water. Bring to a boil, stirring to dissolve the sugar. Add the peels, reduce the heat to low, and cook, uncovered, stirring occasionally and adjusting the heat to prevent scorching, until the peels are translucent and have absorbed most of the syrup, about 30 minutes. Using a slotted spoon, transfer the peels to paper towels to drain.

Place the remaining 2 cups (14 oz/440 g) sugar on a baking sheet. Working in batches, toss the peels in the sugar. Transfer the peels to a sheet of waxed paper, spacing them so they do not touch. Let the candied peels dry for 1–2 hours. Store in layers, separated by waxed paper, in an airtight container at room temperature for up to 1 month.

Makes about 1¼ cups (7½ oz/235 g)

Citrus to try

You can vary the flavors of your candied peel by using almost any type of citrus fruit, from ordinary to exotic. Stick with the delicious basics called for here, or seek out more unusual, aromatic fruits such as bergamot oranges (most familiar as the flavoring for Earl Grey tea), citrons, mandarins, or Meyer lemons.

Sweet ideas

Candied citrus peel makes a tangy topping for ice cream or a pretty garnish for a cake. You can add chopped candied peel to cake batter or scone or cookie dough. To dress up candied grapefruit or orange peel, dip each piece into melted bittersweet chocolate and place on wire racks until the chocolate sets. Serve over ice cream or as a nibble at a cocktail party.

Make it a gift

Sparkling and sweet, candied citrus peel is a festive gift and perfect for the holidays. Layer slices of the candied peel with waxed paper in a glass jar or metal tin or canister. Tie with a decorative ribbon and a small ornament. Include storage information, serving ideas, or a recipe on the gift tag.

This conserve makes a lovely accompaniment to cheese and crackers and is delicious on a ham sandwich. Avoid using overripe peaches, as the fruit needs to stand up to the texture of the nuts and dried fruit. You can substitute nectarines for the peaches.

Peach-Almond Conserve

Have ready hot, sterilized jars and their lids (see page 228).

Using a vegetable peeler, remove the zest from the orange half in long strips about 1 inch (2.5 cm) wide. Remove as much pith as possible from the strips and then cut them crosswise into very thin strips. Set aside.

In a large nonreactive saucepan, combine the peaches and sugar and toss gently. Add the lemon juice, cherries, and apricots. Bring to a simmer over medium heat and cook, uncovered, stirring occasionally, for about 10 minutes. Add the almonds and orange zest and cook for 5 minutes longer. Stir in the almond extract, if using.

Ladle the hot conserve into the jars, leaving ¼ inch (6 mm) of headspace. Remove any air bubbles and adjust the headspace, if necessary. Wipe the rims clean and seal tightly with the lids.

Process the jars for 10 minutes in a boiling-water bath (for detailed instructions, including cooling and testing seals, see pages 228–229). The sealed jars can be stored in a cool, dark place for up to 1 year. If a seal has failed, store the jar in the refrigerator for up to 1 month.

½ orange

3 lb (1.5 kg) peaches, fuzz gently rubbed from the skins, halved, pitted, and cut into ¾-inch (2-cm) chunks (about 10 cups)

1½ cups (12 oz/375 g) sugar

½ cup (4 fl oz/125 ml) fresh lemon juice

½ cup (3 oz/90 g) dried pitted sweet cherries, roughly chopped

1 cup (6 oz/185 g) chopped dried apricots

1 cup (4½ oz/140 g) slivered blanched almonds

¾ tsp almond extract (optional)

Makes 6 half-pint (8–fl oz/250-ml) jars

The flavors of autumn are captured in this chunky fruit conserve. A pinch of ground cinnamon, star anise, or even cloves can be added for extra spice. Serve with roast pork or poultry, or on a cheese plate with a nutty bread, blue cheese, and aged Cheddar.

Pear & Dried Fruit Conserve

Have ready hot, sterilized jars and their lids (see page 228).

In a large nonreactive saucepan, combine the pears, sugar, lemon juice, cranberries, dates, persimmons, walnuts, orange zest, and cardamom. Scrape the seeds from the vanilla bean into the pan and add the pod. Bring to a simmer over medium-high heat and cook, stirring constantly, until most of the liquid has evaporated, about 10 minutes.

Ladle the hot conserve into the jars, leaving ¼ inch (6 mm) of headspace. Remove any air bubbles and adjust the headspace, if necessary. Wipe the rims clean and seal tightly with the lids.

Process the jars for 10 minutes in a boiling-water bath (for detailed instructions, including cooling and testing seals, see pages 228–229). The sealed jars can be stored in a cool, dark place for up to 1 year. If a seal has failed, store the jar in the refrigerator for up to 1 month.

3 lb (1.5 kg) pears such as Warren or Comice, peeled, cored, and cut into ½-inch (12-mm) cubes (about 8 cups)

1 cup (8 oz/250 g) sugar

¼ cup (2 fl oz/60 ml) fresh lemon juice

½ cup (2 oz/60 g) dried cranberries

¼ cup (1½ oz/45 g) chopped dates

¼ cup (1½ oz/45 g) chopped dried persimmons

½ cup (2 oz/60 g) chopped walnuts

Grated zest of ½ orange

¼ tsp ground cardamom

½ vanilla bean, halved lengthwise

Makes 4 half-pint (8–fl oz/250-ml) jars

SWEET BUTTERS & CURDS

"I love to garden, and preserving to me is a natural extension of that. I pick plums from the tree in our yard and make plum butter, which is a staple at our breakfast table all year long. For me, that is pure satisfaction."

LISA ATWOOD

APPLES • PLUMS • PEACHES • PUMPKINS • PEARS • LEMONS • LIMES

Glossy fruit butters, made by slowly simmering puréed fruit until it is reduced to a thick, creamy texture, take longer to cook than other fruit spreads, but are worth the extra time. Apple butter is the best known of the clan, but nearly any type of fruit can be made into a butter, from plums, peaches, and apricots to pears and pumpkins. All of them benefit from the addition of one or more spices and/or fresh herbs to enhance their flavor.

Sweet-tart fruit curds are also thick and creamy, but they depend on a trio of kitchen staples—butter, sugar, and eggs—for their decadently smooth, rich character. Lemons, limes, or other citrus traditionally form the base, though fruits such as berries or melons are also sometimes used. These intensely flavored curds are wildly versatile, too, good spread on warm scones or used as a filling in any number of desserts, from tartlets to layer cakes to a showstopping Pavlova.

Less time-consuming to make, but no less creamy and smooth, are savory spreads made from sweet dairy butter and fresh herbs, citrus peel, or spices. They, too, are versatile, ideal for melting over roasted vegetables or fish, or spreading on biscuits.

Traditional recipes like this one come in handy during apple-picking season. As the mixture slowly cooks down, the sugar caramelizes and the apple butter turns a deep golden brown. Be sure to keep an eye on the butter as it cooks to avoid scorching.

Classic Apple Butter

Have ready hot, sterilized jars and their lids (see page 228).

Peel, quarter, and core the apples. In a large nonreactive saucepan, combine the apples, cider, and lemon juice. Add ½ cup (4 fl oz/125 ml) water and bring to a boil over medium-high heat. Reduce the heat to low, cover, and simmer, stirring occasionally, until the apples are soft, about 30 minutes.

Working in batches if necessary, transfer the apple mixture to a food processor and purée just until smooth. Return to the saucepan and stir in the sugar, cinnamon, and cloves. Place over medium-low heat and cook, uncovered, stirring frequently and scraping down the sides of the pan, until the butter is thick and mounds on a spoon, about 1 hour.

Ladle the hot butter into the jars, leaving ¼ inch (6 mm) of headspace. Remove any air bubbles and adjust the headspace, if necessary. Wipe the rims clean and seal tightly with the lids.

Process the jars for 10 minutes in a boiling-water bath (for detailed instructions, including cooling and testing seals, see pages 228–229). The sealed jars can be stored in a cool, dark place for up to 1 year. If a seal has failed, store the jar in the refrigerator for up to 2 months.

4 lb (2 kg) sweet apples such as Fuji, Gala, Empire, or Pink Lady

1½ cups (12 fl oz/375 ml) sweet apple cider

Juice of 1 lemon

2 cups (1 lb/500 g) sugar

2 tsp ground cinnamon

½ tsp ground cloves

Makes 5 half-pint (8-fl oz/250-ml) jars

The full, sweet flavor of summer peaches picked at season's height needs little embellishment. Use a food mill to remove any stringy pulp and a blender to purée the butter to a silky smoothness. The lemongrass in the variation adds an herbal, lemony essence.

Summer Peach Butter

Have ready hot, sterilized jars and their lids (see page 228).

Blanch and peel the peaches (see page 234), then halve them and remove the pits. Cut the peach halves lengthwise into quarters.

In a large nonreactive saucepan, combine the peaches and lemon juice and toss to coat the peaches. Add ½ cup (4 fl oz/125 ml) water and bring to a boil over medium-high heat. Reduce the heat to medium-low and simmer, covered, stirring occasionally, until the peaches are almost tender, about 20 minutes. Uncover and cook, stirring occasionally, for 10 minutes longer to reduce the liquid slightly.

Working in batches if necessary, pass the peaches through a food mill or fine-mesh sieve set over a bowl. Transfer to a blender and process until smooth. Measure the purée and return to the pan. Stir in enough sugar to equal half the amount of purée. Bring to a boil over medium-high heat, reduce the heat to medium-low, and simmer, uncovered, stirring frequently and scraping down the sides of the pan, until the butter is thick and mounds on a spoon, 1–1½ hours.

Ladle the hot butter into the jars, leaving ¼ inch (6 mm) of headspace. Remove any air bubbles and adjust the headspace, if necessary. Wipe the rims clean and seal tightly with the lids.

Process the jars for 10 minutes in a boiling-water bath (for detailed instructions, including cooling and testing seals, see pages 228–229). The sealed jars can be stored in a cool, dark place for up to 1 year. If a seal has failed, store the jar in the refrigerator for up to 2 months.

6 lb (3 kg) peaches

1 Tbsp fresh lemon juice

About 3½ cups (1¾ lb/875 g) sugar

Makes 6 half-pint (8–fl oz/250-ml) jars

Peach-Lemongrass Butter
Cut 6 thick lemongrass stalks, white parts only, into 2-inch (5-cm) pieces and crush with a meat pounder. Add to the quartered peaches and cook as directed. Before puréeing the peaches, remove and discard the larger pieces of lemongrass. Smaller pieces will be removed by the food mill. Cook the purée as directed.

Achieving the correct viscosity for this butter can be tricky, since the cooking time varies according to the ripeness of the plums. After the butter is simmered, it should have the thickness of heavy (double) cream, and once it cools a bit, it should drip thickly from a spoon.

Plum Butter

Have ready hot, sterilized jars and their lids (see page 228).

Using a vegetable peeler, cut 4 strips of zest from the orange, each about 1 inch (2.5 cm) wide and 4 inches (10 cm) long. Cut the orange in half and squeeze enough juice to measure ¼ cup (2 fl oz/60 ml). Pour into a large nonreactive saucepan.

Halve and pit each plum, and cut each half into 3 pieces. Place the pieces in the saucepan, add the sugar, and stir gently to combine. Bring to a boil over medium-high heat, stirring to dissolve the sugar. Reduce the heat to medium and simmer, uncovered, stirring often, until the plums are tender, about 5 minutes.

Working in batches if necessary, pass the plums through a food mill or fine-mesh sieve set over another large nonreactive saucepan. Stir in the vanilla and cinnamon and bring to a boil over medium-high heat. Reduce the heat to low and simmer, uncovered, stirring frequently, until the butter is the consistency of heavy cream, 55–70 minutes.

Ladle the hot butter into the jars, leaving ¼ inch (6 mm) of headspace. Remove any air bubbles and adjust the headspace, if necessary. Wipe the rims clean and seal tightly with the lids.

Process the jars for 10 minutes in a boiling-water bath (for detailed instructions, including cooling and testing seals, see pages 228–229). The sealed jars can be stored in a cool, dark place for up to 1 year. If a seal has failed, store the jar in the refrigerator for up to 2 months.

1 orange

4 lb (2 kg) plums

3¼ cups (26 oz/815 g) sugar

½ tsp pure vanilla extract

½ tsp ground cinnamon

Makes 5 half-pint (8–fl oz/250-ml) jars

Pumpkins are a sure sign of autumn. Sugar pumpkins are a good choice here, but also look for heirloom varieties at farmers' markets. The best have firm, flavorful, and nearly string-free flesh. For safety reasons, this butter should be refrigerated or frozen (not canned).

Spiced Pumpkin Butter

Have ready hot, sterilized jars and their lids (see page 228), unless you plan on freezing the butter (see below).

Preheat the oven to 425°F (220°C). Cut each pumpkin in half. Scoop out and discard the seeds. Brush the pumpkin halves with the melted butter and place, cut side down, on a baking sheet. Bake until tender, 25–35 minutes, depending on the size of the pumpkin halves. Using a spoon, scoop the flesh from the pumpkin halves and place in a bowl. Stir and mash the pumpkin until puréed. Measure out 5 cups (2½ lb/1.25 kg) of the pumpkin purée; reserve any remaining purée for another use.

In a large nonreactive saucepan, combine the pumpkin purée, sugars, cider, ginger, cinnamon, nutmeg, and cloves. Stir until blended. Bring just to a boil over medium-high heat, stirring constantly. Reduce the heat to medium-low and cook, uncovered, stirring frequently and scraping down the sides of the pan, until the butter is thick and mounds on a spoon, about 30 minutes.

Ladle the hot butter into the jars, leaving ¼ inch (6 mm) of headspace. Remove any air bubbles and adjust the headspace, if necessary. Wipe the rims clean and seal tightly with the lids. The sealed jars can be stored in the refrigerator for up to 2 months. The butter can also be stored in airtight containers or heavy-duty resealable plastic bags in the freezer for up to 1 year.

2 small pumpkins, about 4 lb (2 kg) each

2 Tbsp unsalted butter, melted

2 cups (1 lb/500 g) granulated sugar

1 cup (7 oz/220 g) firmly packed light brown sugar

1½ cups (12 fl oz/375 ml) sweet apple cider

3½ tsp ground ginger

3½ tsp ground cinnamon

1½ tsp ground nutmeg

½ tsp ground cloves

Makes 6 half-pint (8–fl oz/250-ml) jars

Fragrant and tasty, this bread puts the deliciously spicy pumpkin butter to good use. The recipe makes two generous loaves, so you can freeze one to eat later. Let the extra loaf cool completely, wrap it in plastic wrap, then in aluminum foil, and freeze for up to 2 months.

Spiced Pumpkin Butter Bread

Preheat the oven to 350°F (180°C). Butter two 9-by-5-inch (23-by-13-cm) loaf pans and then dust with flour, tapping out the excess.

In a bowl, whisk together the flour, baking soda, salt, and baking powder. In a large bowl, combine the pumpkin butter, sugar, oil, eggs, vanilla, and ½ cup (4 fl oz/125 ml) water. Stir until well mixed. Stir in the walnuts, if using. Gradually add the flour mixture to the pumpkin mixture and stir just until blended. Divide the batter between the pans.

Bake until a toothpick inserted into the center of each loaf comes out clean, 45–50 minutes. Let the loaves cool in the pans on wire racks for 10 minutes. Unmold the loaves onto the racks, arrange them upright, and let cool completely. Cut into slices to serve.

3½ cups (17½ oz/545 g) all-purpose (plain) flour

2 tsp baking soda (bicarbonate of soda)

1½ tsp salt

1 tsp baking powder

2 cups (1 lb/500 g) Spiced Pumpkin Butter (facing page)

1¼ cups (10 oz/315 g) sugar

1 cup (8 fl oz/250 ml) canola oil

4 eggs, at room temperature

1 tsp pure vanilla extract

1 cup (4 oz/125 g) chopped walnuts (optional)

Makes two 9-by-5-inch (23-by-13-cm) loaves

Savory Butters

You'll be amazed at how simple it is to turn an ordinary stick of butter into something spectacular, drawing on fresh herbs or other flavorings from your garden and pantry.

Ingredients to Try

Experiment with different flavor combinations for savory butters. Among the delicious options are minced garlic or shallots; chopped capers or sun-dried tomatoes; chopped fresh herbs, such as rosemary, basil, parsley, or tarragon; finely grated citrus zest; and fresh edible flowers like nasturtiums or violets.

How to Make

Combine the butter and the flavorings (see ideas at right) in a food processor. Process until thoroughly combined and smooth. Alternatively, use a spoon to beat together all the ingredients in a small bowl until completely mixed. Transfer the butter to a sheet of waxed paper or plastic wrap. Shape the butter into a log about 2 inches (5 cm) in diameter, rolling the paper around the butter to enclose completely. Twist the paper at the ends of the log to secure. Refrigerate for up to 1 week, or place in a heavy-duty resealable plastic bag and freeze for up to 9 months. Bring to room temperature before serving.

Ways to Use

Flavored butters add the perfect finishing touch to countless dishes. Adorn a simply grilled steak with a pat of tarragon-mustard butter. Spread chile-lime butter on corn on the cob, or place a disk atop a salmon steak fresh off a charcoal fire. Top a baked potato with rosemary-shallot butter, or stir it into mashed potatoes. Toss pasta with garlic-basil butter. Use nasturtium–sea salt butter to make canapés: spread on mini toasts or brioche rounds and top with cucumbers and/or smoked salmon.

Garlic-basil

Combine ½ cup (4 oz/125 g) unsalted butter, at room temperature; 2 Tbsp finely chopped fresh basil; 1 Tbsp minced garlic; and ½ tsp coarse salt.

Rosemary-shallot

Combine ½ cup (4 oz/125 g) unsalted butter, at room temperature; 2 Tbsp minced shallots; 1 Tbsp chopped fresh rosemary; and ½ tsp *each* coarse salt and freshly ground pepper.

Chile-lime

Combine ½ cup (4 oz/125 g) unsalted butter, at room temperature; grated zest of 1 lime; ½ tsp chile powder; and ½ tsp coarse salt.

Nasturtium–sea salt

Combine ½ cup (4 oz/125 g) unsalted butter, at room temperature; 2 Tbsp chopped organic nasturtium flowers; 1 Tbsp snipped fresh chives; and ½ tsp coarse sea salt.

Tarragon-mustard

Combine ½ cup (4 oz/125 g) unsalted butter, at room temperature; 2 Tbsp chopped fresh tarragon; 2 Tbsp Dijon mustard; and ¼ tsp *each* coarse salt and freshly ground pepper.

This sweet spread, infused with a hint of cardamom, is smooth and delicate. The addition of orange juice and citrus zest tempers the sweetness of the pears. Spoon it on toasted brioche in the morning, or pair it with a tangy sheep's milk cheese or a small wedge of blue cheese.

Pear-Cardamom Butter

Have ready hot, sterilized jars and their lids (see page 228).

Quarter and core the pears. In a large nonreactive saucepan, combine the pears and the lemon juice and toss to coat. Add ½ cup (4 fl oz/125 ml) water and bring to a boil over high heat. Reduce the heat to medium-low, cover, and simmer, stirring once or twice, until the pears are tender, about 20 minutes. Remove from the heat and let cool slightly.

Working in batches if necessary, pass the pears through a food mill or fine-mesh sieve set over a bowl. Transfer to a food processor and purée just until smooth. Return to the saucepan. Stir in the sugar, orange juice, orange and lemon zest, cardamom, and vanilla. Bring to a boil over medium-high heat, reduce the heat to medium, and simmer, uncovered, stirring frequently and scraping down the sides of the pan, until the butter is thick and mounds on a spoon, about 1 hour. Remove and discard the zest strips.

Ladle the hot butter into the jars, leaving ¼ inch (6 mm) of headspace. Remove any air bubbles and adjust the headspace, if necessary. Wipe the rims clean and seal tightly with the lids.

Process the jars for 10 minutes in a boiling-water bath (for detailed instructions, including cooling and testing seals, see pages 228–229). The sealed jars can be stored in a cool, dark place for up to 1 year. If a seal has failed, store the jar in the refrigerator for up to 2 months.

4 lb (2 kg) pears, preferably Bartlett (Williams')

2 Tbsp fresh lemon juice

1½ cups (12 oz/375 g) sugar

¼ cup (2 fl oz/60 ml) fresh orange juice

2 orange zest strips, each about 1 inch (2.5 cm) wide and 4 inches (10 cm) long and studded with 2 whole cloves

2 lemon zest strips, each about ½ inch (12 mm) wide and 1 inch (2.5 cm) long

1 tsp ground cardamom

½ tsp pure vanilla extract

Makes 6 half-pint (8–fl oz/250-ml) jars

Smooth and creamy, this bright, citrusy fruit spread is both sweet and tart. Substituting Meyer lemons makes for a slightly sweeter flavor. The curd is versatile, perfect for filling tarts or sandwich cookies, spreading between cake layers, or slathering on scones at teatime.

Lemon Curd

Have ready hot, sterilized jars and their lids (see page 228).

Finely grate the zest from 1 of the lemons. Cut all of the lemons in half and squeeze enough juice to measure ⅓ cup (3 fl oz/80 ml).

In a nonreactive heatproof bowl set over (not touching) simmering water, whisk together the lemon zest and juice, sugar, and eggs. While stirring constantly, add the butter, a few cubes at a time, letting the cubes melt before adding more and scraping the bottom of the bowl each time. Cook, whisking, just until the mixture has thickened enough to coat the back of a spoon, 10–15 minutes. Do not let the mixture boil.

Ladle the hot curd into the jars, leaving ¼ inch (6 mm) of headspace. Remove any air bubbles and adjust the headspace if necessary. Wipe the rims clean and seal tightly with lids. Set aside to cool completely, about 30 minutes. The curd can be stored in the refrigerator for up to 2 weeks.

2 or 3 lemons

½ cup (4 oz/125 g) sugar

3 eggs, lightly beaten

½ cup (4 oz/125 g) unsalted butter, cut into small cubes

Makes 2 half-pint (8–fl oz/250-ml) jars

For an easy dessert, fill a gingersnap crust with your favorite citrus curd. The spicy, buttery crust is a perfect foil for the curd's tangy flavor and smooth texture. You can make tartlets or one large tart. Garnish either size with fresh fruit and a scattering of zest.

Lemon Curd Tartlets

Preheat the oven to 375°F (190°C). Butter four 4½-inch (11.5-cm) tartlet pans with removable bottoms.

To make the crust, in a food processor, combine the gingersnap crumbs and butter. Pulse until the butter is evenly distributed and the mixture starts to clump together. Remove from the food processor and press the mixture onto the bottom and up the sides of the prepared tartlet pans.

Bake until the crusts are set and begin to brown, 8–10 minutes. Transfer to a wire rack and let cool.

Remove the cooled tartlet shells from the pans and gently spoon the curd into the shells. Arrange the kiwifruit slices on top, garnish with the lemon zest, and serve.

FOR THE CRUST

1¾ cups (5 oz/155 g) gingersnap crumbs

5 Tbsp (2½ oz/75 g) unsalted butter, at room temperature

About 1½ cups (12 fl oz/ 375 ml) Lemon Curd (page 109)

3 or 4 kiwifruits, peeled and thinly sliced

1 Tbsp grated lemon zest

Makes 4 tartlets

The term "tangerine" is typically used for any mandarin orange with a deep-colored skin. If tangerines are unavailable, you can substitute tangelos, which are a cross between a mandarin and a grapefruit or pomelo. Lemon juice is added to give this curd some extra zing.

Tangerine Curd

Have ready hot, sterilized jars and their lids (see page 228).

Finely grate the zest from the tangerines. Cut the tangerines in half and squeeze enough juice to measure about 3 cups (24 fl oz/750 ml). In a nonreactive saucepan, combine the tangerine zest and juice and the lemon juice. Bring to a boil and cook, stirring occasionally, until reduced to ¾ cup (6 fl oz/180 ml), about 20 minutes. Let cool.

In a nonreactive heatproof bowl set over (not touching) simmering water, whisk together the whole eggs, egg yolks, sugar, and reduced juice and zest mixture. While stirring constantly, add the butter, a few cubes at a time, letting the cubes melt before adding more and scraping the bottom of the bowl each time. Cook, whisking, just until the mixture has thickened enough to coat the back of a spoon, about 10 minutes. Do not let the mixture boil.

Ladle the hot curd into the jars, leaving ¼ inch (6 mm) of headspace. Remove any air bubbles and adjust the headspace if necessary. Wipe the rims clean and seal tightly with lids. Set aside to cool completely, about 30 minutes. The curd can be stored in the refrigerator for up to 2 weeks.

2½ lb (1.25 kg) tangerines

½ cup (4 fl oz/125 ml) fresh lemon juice

3 whole eggs plus 2 egg yolks, lightly beaten

½ cup (4 oz/125 g) sugar

⅔ cup (5 oz/155 g) unsalted butter, cut into small cubes

Makes 3 half-pint (8–fl oz/250-ml) jars

A quintessential British teatime combination, scones and curd belong together. To ensure tender scones, use a light touch, work quickly, and put them into the oven right after cutting. Just before baking, add a glaze of cream and a sprinkle of Demerara sugar for golden tops.

Currant Scones with Tangerine Curd

Preheat the oven to 375°F (190°C). Butter a baking sheet and then dust with flour, tapping out the excess.

In a bowl, sift together the flour, baking powder, salt, and sugar. Using your fingertips, rub in the butter until the mixture resembles fine meal. Stir in the currants. Make a well in the center of the flour mixture and pour in the half-and-half. Using a rubber spatula, quickly mix together to form a soft dough. Do not overmix.

Turn out the dough onto a lightly floured work surface and cut in half. Lightly form each half into a round about ½ inch (12 mm) thick. Using a sharp knife, cut each round into 10 equal wedges. Transfer the wedges to the prepared baking sheet.

Bake until the scones are golden brown, 15–17 minutes. Transfer to a wire rack and let cool for a few minutes. Serve warm with the curd.

2 cups (10 oz/315 g) all-purpose (plain) flour

1 tsp baking powder

¼ tsp salt

⅓ cup (3 oz/90 g) sugar

¼ cup (2 oz/60 g) cold unsalted butter, cut into small pieces

½ cup (3 oz/90 g) dried currants

½ cup (4 fl oz/125 ml) half-and-half (half cream)

Tangerine Curd (page 112) for serving

Makes 20 scones

A nice alternative to classic lemon curd, lime provides a punchier flavor and a brighter color. It pairs well with berries and meringue or whipped cream, making it a good filling for tarts, a welcome layer in parfaits, or an ideal topping for a Pavlova (page 116).

Lime Curd

Have ready hot, sterilized jars and their lids (see page 228).

Finely grate the zest from 3 of the limes. Cut the limes in half and squeeze enough juice to measure ½ cup (4 fl oz/125 ml), using the additional limes if necessary.

In a nonreactive heatproof bowl set over (not touching) simmering water, whisk together the sugar, eggs, and lime zest and juice. While stirring constantly, add the butter, a few cubes at a time, letting the cubes melt before adding more and scraping the bottom of the bowl each time. Cook, whisking, just until the mixture has thickened enough to coat the back of a spoon, 10–15 minutes. Do not let the mixture boil.

Ladle the hot curd into the jars, leaving ¼ inch (6 mm) of headspace. Remove any air bubbles and adjust the headspace if necessary. Wipe the rims clean and seal tightly with lids. Set aside to cool completely, about 30 minutes. The curd can be stored in the refrigerator for up to 2 weeks.

4 or 5 limes

1 cup (8 oz/250 g) sugar

4 eggs, lightly beaten

¾ cup (6 oz/185 g) plus 2 Tbsp butter, cut into small cubes

Makes 2 half-pint (8–fl oz/250-ml) jars

This meringue dessert, named after Russian ballerina Anna Pavlova, has a crisp crust and soft, sometimes chewy interior. Lime curd, or any citrus curd, offsets the sweet meringue and delivers a smooth texture. Garnish with whipped cream and a mix of fresh berries.

Pavlova with Lime Curd & Berries

Position a rack in the lower third of the oven and preheat to 300°F (150°C). Draw a 9-inch (23-cm) circle on a sheet of parchment (baking) paper. Turn the parchment paper over and place on a baking sheet.

In a bowl, using an electric mixer on medium speed, beat the egg whites until well mixed. Sprinkle the cornstarch over the whites and continue to beat until the whites are white and foamy. Raise the speed to high and very gradually add the sugar, beating until stiff, shiny peaks form. Quickly beat in the lemon juice and vanilla. Spread the meringue inside the circle drawn on the parchment, building up the edges slightly to form a rim.

Bake until the meringue is crispy, about 40 minutes. Turn off the oven and open the door. When the meringue is completely cool, remove it from the oven. Remove the meringue from the parchment paper and place on a serving plate.

Using the electric mixer, chilled clean beaters, and a chilled bowl, whip the cream until stiff peaks form. Spread the curd in the hollow of the meringue. Top with half of the whipped cream and sprinkle with the berries. Let stand for 10 minutes to soften the center of the meringue slightly. Cut into wedges and serve, passing the remaining whipped cream at the table.

4 egg whites

1 Tbsp cornstarch (cornflour)

1 cup (8 oz/250 g) sugar

1 tsp fresh lemon juice

1 tsp pure vanilla extract

1 cup (8 fl oz/250 ml) heavy (double) cream

1½ cups (12 fl oz/375 ml) Lime Curd (page 115)

3 cups (12 oz/375 g) mixed berries

Serves 6–8

PICKLED FRUITS & VEGETABLES

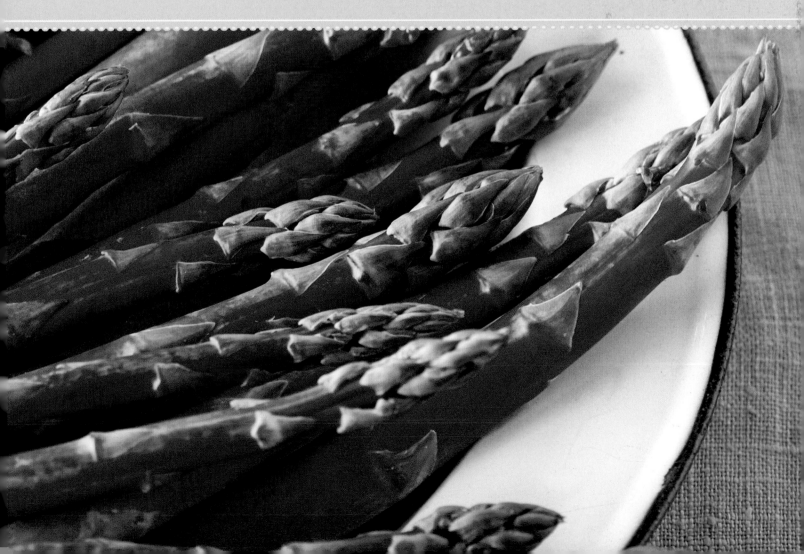

"Growing up, my family spent many an evening pickling all the produce that teemed from our garden. We had our favorites: dill pickles, pickled green tomatoes, and pickled string beans that we called dilly beans."

RICK FIELD

CUCUMBERS • FENNEL • ASPARAGUS • RHUBARB • PEPPERS • OKRA

Old-fashioned pickling—fruits or vegetables preserved in a brine composed of an acid (such as vinegar), salt, and a mix of spices—has found new enthusiasts in the contemporary kitchen. Cucumbers of every variety are the most commonly pickled items, but don't stop there. Almost any vegetable or fruit, from green tomatoes, okra, and Brussels sprouts to asparagus and rhubarb, can be used, making pickling a solution for bumper crops from your garden or a local farmers' market.

All kinds of fresh herbs and spices—peppercorns, anise, dill fronds, mustard seeds, fennel—can be added to the brine to impart subtle flavor or a spicy kick to whatever you are pickling. Preserved lemons boast their own unique formula: the fruits are packed with plenty of their juice and lots of salt. When they are ready, you discard the pulp and use the peel to flavor a chicken as it roasts or to add a salty tang to a salad.

Indeed, all of these savory pickles are remarkably adaptable, working equally well as a condiment or garnish, as an addition to sandwiches and salads, or as the centerpiece of a cheese plate or antipasto platter.

Some things, like these crisp dill pickles, are classic for a reason. If you are new to pickling vegetables, start with this straightforward recipe. Make the pickles at the height of summer, when small Kirby cucumbers and heads of fresh dill can be found at local farmers' markets.

Classic Dill Pickles

Have ready hot, sterilized jars and their lids (see page 228).

In a large nonreactive saucepan, combine the vinegar and salt. Add 3 cups (24 fl oz/750 ml) water and bring to a boil over medium-high heat, stirring to dissolve the salt.

Meanwhile, in each jar, place 1 Tbsp pickling spice, 1 dill head (or 1 Tbsp dill seeds and 4 dill sprigs), 4 garlic cloves, and 6 peppercorns. Layer the cucumber slices in the jars, making sure to pack them tightly and avoid large gaps. Fill the jars to within ¾ inch (2 cm) of the rims.

Ladle the hot brine into the jars, leaving ½ inch (12 mm) of headspace. Remove any air bubbles and adjust the headspace, if necessary. Wipe the rims clean and seal tightly with the lids.

Process the jars for 7 minutes in a boiling-water bath (for detailed instructions, including cooling and testing seals, see pages 228–229). Let the jars stand undisturbed for 24 hours and then set them aside for 2 weeks for the flavors to develop. The sealed jars can be stored in a cool, dark place for up to 1 year. If a seal has failed, store the jar in the refrigerator for up to 1 week.

3 cups (24 fl oz/750 ml) distilled white vinegar (5 percent acidity)

2 Tbsp kosher salt

6 Tbsp (1½ oz/45 g) pickling spice (page 19 or purchased)

6 large, mature dill heads, or 6 Tbsp (1½ oz/45 g) dill seeds and 24 fresh dill sprigs

24 cloves garlic

36 peppercorns

6 lb (3 kg) Kirby cucumbers, each about 1½ inches (4 cm) in diameter, cut into slices ½ inch (12 mm) thick

Makes 6 one-pint (16–fl oz/500-ml) jars

Dried cherries and modest amounts of red pepper and turmeric tame the overwhelming sweetness found in many standard recipes for these pickles. Prepare them at the beginning of the summer so you will have them on hand for a season's worth of barbecues.

Bread & Butter Pickles

In a large nonreactive bowl, combine the cucumber and onion slices. Add 1 Tbsp of the salt and the ice cubes. Cover and refrigerate for 3–4 hours. Drain in a colander, rinse, and then set aside to drain well.

Have ready hot, sterilized jars and their lids (see page 228).

In a large nonreactive saucepan, combine the vinegar, sugar, turmeric, cherries, and remaining 2 Tbsp plus 1 tsp salt. Add 1½ cups (12 fl oz/ 375 ml) plus 2 Tbsp water and bring to a boil over medium-high heat, stirring to dissolve the salt.

Meanwhile, place the cucumbers and onion in a large bowl. Add the mustard and celery seeds and the red pepper flakes and stir to combine. Using a slotted spoon, remove the cherries from the brine, transfer to the bowl, and stir to combine with the vegetables. Pack the cucumber mixture into the jars as tightly as possible. Fill the jars to within ½ inch (12 mm) of the rims.

Ladle the hot brine into the jars, leaving ½ inch of headspace. Remove any air bubbles and adjust the headspace, if necessary. Wipe the rims clean and seal tightly with the lids.

Process the jars for 7 minutes in a boiling-water bath (for detailed instructions, including cooling and testing seals, see pages 228–229). Let the jars stand undisturbed for 24 hours and then set them aside for 2 weeks for the flavors to develop. The sealed jars can be stored in a cool, dark place for up to 1 year. If a seal has failed, store the jar in the refrigerator for up to 1 week.

6 lb (3 kg) Kirby cucumbers, each about 1½ inches (4 cm) in diameter, cut into slices ¼ inch (6 mm) thick

1 yellow onion, cut into slices ¼ inch (6 mm) thick

3 Tbsp plus 1 tsp kosher salt

6 ice cubes

4 cups (32 fl oz/1 l) cider vinegar (5 percent acidity)

¼ cup (2 oz/60 g) plus 1 Tbsp sugar

1 tsp ground turmeric

½ cup (3 oz/90 g) dried pitted sour cherries

2 tsp mustard seeds

1 tsp celery seeds

½ tsp red pepper flakes

Makes 6 one-pint (16–fl oz/500-ml) jars

Pickled beets charm in salad preparations, lending color, texture, and their signature flavor. Try them layered with fresh mozzarella and a drizzle of olive oil, or eat them straight from the jar. Any beet variety, from red to gold to red-and-white-striped Chioggias, can be used.

Pickled Beets

Have ready hot, sterilized jars and their lids (see page 228).

Put the beets into a large saucepan (if using different-colored beets, separate them into 2 saucepans) and add water to cover by 2 inches (5 cm). Bring to a boil, reduce the heat to medium-low, cover partially, and simmer until the beets are tender, 25–30 minutes. Drain the beets, reserving 2 cups (16 fl oz/500 ml) of the cooking liquid.

When the cooked beets are cool enough to handle, peel them and then cut into slices ¼ inch (6 mm) thick. Divide the beet slices and the onion slices among the jars.

In a saucepan over medium heat, combine the reserved cooking liquid, the vinegar, sugar, cardamom, cloves, and salt. Bring to a boil, stirring, just until the sugar is dissolved.

Ladle the hot vinegar mixture into the jars, evenly distributing the spices and leaving ½ inch (12 mm) of headspace. Remove any air bubbles and adjust the headspace, if necessary. Wipe the rims clean and seal tightly with the lids.

Process the jars for 7 minutes in a boiling-water bath (for detailed instructions, including cooling and testing seals, see pages 228–229). Let the jars stand undisturbed for 24 hours and then set them aside for 1 week for the flavors to develop. The sealed jars can be stored in a cool, dark place for up to 3 months. If a seal has failed, store the jar in the refrigerator for up to 1 week.

1 lb (500 g) beets

1 white onion, sliced

1 cup (8 fl oz/250 ml) cider vinegar (5 percent acidity)

¼ cup (2 oz/60 g) sugar, or to taste

1 Tbsp cardamom pods

1 Tbsp whole cloves

Pinch of salt

Makes 4 one-pint (16–fl oz/500-ml) jars

Pickled beets give this salad some extra zing and make for a gorgeous presentation. Minced preserved lemon, deliciously salty and citrusy at the same time, is a great addition to salad dressings. Crumbled fresh goat cheese or feta can be substituted for the ricotta salata.

Arugula & Pickled Beet Salad

To make the croutons, if using, cut the bread slices into 1-inch (2.5-cm) cubes. In a frying pan over medium heat, warm the olive oil. Add the bread cubes, reduce the heat to low, and cook, turning once, until golden and crusty, about 4 minutes on each side. Sprinkle with the salt and thyme, toss briefly, and transfer to paper towels to drain.

In a large bowl, whisk together the vinegar, mustard, pepper, and lemon. Gradually whisk in the olive oil until smooth. Add the arugula and beets and toss to coat well.

Divide the salad among individual plates. Using a vegetable peeler, shave the ricotta salata over the salads. Serve at once.

FOR THE CROUTONS (OPTIONAL)

6 slices day-old baguette, each 1 inch (2.5 cm) thick

2 Tbsp olive oil

¼ tsp sea salt

2 tsp minced fresh thyme

2 Tbsp white wine vinegar

1 tsp Dijon mustard (page 194 or purchased)

½ tsp freshly ground pepper

½ Preserved Lemon (page 130), peel only, minced

⅓ cup (3 fl oz/80 ml) olive oil

4 cups (4 oz/125 g) arugula (rocket)

1 cup (6 oz/185 g) Pickled Beets (page 125), slices halved

¼ lb (125 g) ricotta salata cheese

Serves 4

The secret to pickling asparagus is to avoid overwhelming its delicate flavor with strong seasonings. Here, lemon juice and coriander seeds subtly complement the spears. Include them on an antipasto plate or add them to a salad (use a splash of brine in the dressing).

Pickled Asparagus

Have ready hot, sterilized jars and their lids (see page 228).

In a large nonreactive saucepan, combine the vinegar, lemon juice, sugar, and salt. Add 3 cups (24 fl oz/750 ml) water and bring to a boil over medium-high heat, stirring to dissolve the sugar and salt.

Meanwhile, in each jar, put ½ tsp coriander seeds. Trim about 1½ inches (4 cm) from the bottom of each asparagus spear. Cut the spears in half into 4-inch (10-cm) pieces. Pack the asparagus in the jars, evenly distributing the bottom halves with the tips and gently placing the tips down. Pack the asparagus as tightly as possible into the jars to within ¾ inch (2 cm) of the rims.

Ladle the hot brine into the jars, leaving ½ inch (12 mm) of headspace. Remove any air bubbles and adjust the headspace, if necessary. Wipe the rims clean and seal tightly with the lids.

Process the jars for 7 minutes in a boiling-water bath (for detailed instructions, including cooling and testing seals, see pages 228–229). Let the jars stand undisturbed for 24 hours and then set them aside for 2 weeks for the flavors to develop. The sealed jars can be stored in a cool, dark place for up to 1 year. If a seal has failed, store the jar in the refrigerator for up to 1 week.

3 cups (24 fl oz/750 ml) white wine vinegar (6 percent acidity)

½ cup (4 fl oz/125 ml) fresh lemon juice

2 tsp sugar

2 tsp salt

1 Tbsp coriander seeds

4 lb (2 kg) thin asparagus (about 4 bunches), at least 9½ inches (24 cm) long

Makes 6 one-pint (16–fl oz/500-ml) jars

Sweet–tart rhubarb makes an excellent pickle when preserved in a tangy brine with sprightly spices. The crisp rhubarb retains its texture and is quite chewy. If you prefer a softer result, blanch the rhubarb in boiling water for a minute, drain, and let cool before packing in jars.

Pickled Rhubarb

Have ready hot, sterilized jars and their lids (see page 228).

In a large nonreactive saucepan, combine the rice and sherry vinegars, cherry juice, and chili powder. Add 3 cups (24 fl oz/750 ml) water and bring to a boil over medium-high heat.

Meanwhile, place a pinch of ginger slivers and 6 garlic cloves in each jar. Pack the rhubarb pieces snugly into the jars, making sure that none stick up above the fill line.

Ladle the hot brine into the jars, leaving ½ inch (12 mm) of headspace. Remove any air bubbles and adjust the headspace, if necessary. Wipe the rims clean and seal tightly with the lids. Let the jars stand undisturbed for 24 hours and then store in the refrigerator for up to 1 month.

1 cup (8 fl oz/250 ml) rice vinegar, preferably yuzu rice vinegar

1 cup (8 fl oz/250 ml) sherry vinegar (7 percent acidity)

1 cup (8 fl oz/250 ml) unsweetened cherry juice

2 tsp chili powder

1-inch (2.5-cm) piece fresh ginger, peeled and cut into slivers

36 cloves garlic

3 lb (1.5 kg) rhubarb, trimmed and cut into 4-inch (10-cm) pieces

Makes 6 one-pint (16–fl oz/500-ml) jars

Preserved Lemons

A staple in the pantries of the Middle East and North Africa, preserved lemons are a lemon lover's dream. To make preserved limes using the same technique, see page 233.

10 firm, slightly underripe lemons, preferably Meyer lemons

12 Tbsp (6 oz/185 g) kosher salt

3 cups (24 fl oz/750 ml) fresh lemon juice, or as needed

Have ready hot, sterilized jars and their lids (see page 228).

In a large nonreactive saucepan, bring 3 qt (3 l) water to a boil. Meanwhile, scrub each lemon thoroughly under cold running water to remove any dirt or wax. Add the lemons to the water, return to a boil, and cook until softened, 3–4 minutes. Remove with a slotted spoon and set aside to cool.

Cut each lemon lengthwise into quarters, leaving them attached at the stem end. Gently spread apart the quarters and sprinkle 1 Tbsp salt into the center. Place 1 Tbsp salt in each jar and pack the lemons into the jars. Pour in enough lemon juice to cover the lemons, leaving ½ inch (12 mm) of headspace. Seal the jars tightly.

Store the lemons in a cool, dark place for 3 weeks, turning the jars occasionally to distribute the lemon juice and salt evenly. Preserved lemons can be stored in the refrigerator for up to 6 months.

Makes 2 one-quart (1-l) jars

Choosing lemons

Look for organic, unwaxed lemons, and scrub them thoroughly. Be sure to buy extra lemons for juicing. If Meyer lemons are available, use them for slightly sweeter preserved lemons.

Ways to use

After you've made preserved lemons, you'll have to hold yourself back from trying to incorporate the bright, tangy peel into every dish you make. Add minced peel to vinaigrettes (see page 126) and marinades, or stir the peel into stews. Tuck preserved lemon quarters into a chicken cavity before roasting it (see page 133).

Flavor boosts

If desired, you can further punch up the flavor of preserved lemons by adding any one of the following flavorings, or a combination, to each jar: 2 bay leaves, 2 cinnamon sticks, 1 tsp peppercorns, 4 whole cloves, and 1 or 2 tsp coriander seeds.

Lemons are often used when roasting a chicken. Here, preserved lemons replace fresh ones, with a moist and tangy result. For added flavor, gently separate the skin from the breast before roasting and tuck thin slices of preserved-lemon peel and herb sprigs under the skin.

Roast Chicken with Preserved Lemons & Herbs

Preheat the oven to 350°F (180°C).

Rub the chicken with a lemon quarter and then with the salt, pepper, and chopped herbs. Place 4 of the herb sprigs and all but 6 of the remaining lemon quarters in the cavity. Tie the legs together with kitchen string, and tuck the wing tips under the back. Place the chicken, breast side up, in a roasting pan. Scatter the remaining herb sprigs and lemon quarters in the pan.

Roast the chicken until an instant-read thermometer inserted into the thickest part of a thigh away from the bone registers 165°–170°F (74°–77°C), about 1¼ hours.

Remove the chicken from the oven, tent loosely with aluminum foil, and let stand for 10 minutes. Cut the string from the legs, discard the contents of the cavity, and carve the chicken. Arrange on a warmed platter. Discard the lemon quarters and herb sprigs in the pan. Using a spoon, skim off the excess fat from the pan juices. Drizzle the remaining juices on top of the chicken. Garnish the chicken with the fresh herb sprigs, if using. Serve at once.

1 chicken, about 3 lb (1.5 kg)

4 Preserved Lemons (page 130), quartered lengthwise

1 tsp salt

1 tsp freshly ground pepper

1 Tbsp chopped fresh herbs such as thyme, tarragon, or winter savory

8 fresh herb sprigs such as thyme, tarragon, or winter savory, plus extra sprigs for garnish (optional)

Serves 4

Sourcing fresh olives isn't easy, but here's a simple way to add your own seasonings to store-bought brine-cured olives. Try other flavor variations, from herbs and chiles to stuffings of cheese or anchovies. Serve the olives warm alongside cheese, sliced meats, and crusty bread.

Citrus-Herb Olives

Have ready a hot, sterilized jar and its lid (see page 228).

Pat the olives dry with paper towels. Place on a firm work surface and, using the side of a large knife, crush each olive just until the skin cracks. Place the olives in the jar. Add the lemon zest.

In a small saucepan over medium-low heat, combine the ¾ cup olive oil, the thyme sprigs, garlic, red pepper flakes, and fennel seeds. Bring just to a simmer. Pour over the olives, adding more oil if needed to cover the olives completely. Let stand at room temperature for about 4 hours.

Wipe the rim of the jar and seal tightly with the lid. Refrigerate for at least 2 days for the flavors to develop. The olives can be stored in the refrigerator for up to 2 months.

1½ cups (½ lb/250 g) brine-cured large green olives such as French or Spanish

6 thin lemon or orange zest strips

¾ cup (6 fl oz/180 ml) extra-virgin olive oil, or as needed

3 fresh thyme or rosemary sprigs

1 clove garlic, minced

½ tsp red pepper flakes

½ tsp fennel seeds

Makes 1 one-pint (16–fl oz/500-ml) jar

You can enjoy these spicy beans on their own or use them as a garnish for refreshing Bloody Marys (page 137). Omit the cayenne pepper in favor of some small, fresh chiles, abundant at farmers' markets in late summer. If using cayenne, adjust the heat by altering the amount.

Dilly Beans

Have ready hot, sterilized jars and their lids (see page 228).

In a large nonreactive saucepan, combine the vinegar and salt. Add 3 cups (24 fl oz/750 ml) water and bring to a boil over medium-high heat, stirring to dissolve the salt.

Meanwhile, in each jar, place 1 dill head (or 1 Tbsp dill seeds and 4 dill sprigs), ¼ tsp cayenne, and 1 garlic clove. Trim the beans so they are ½ inch (12 mm) shorter than the height of the jars. Pack the beans as tightly as possible into the jars. It may help to hold the jar horizontally and use a chopstick to compact the beans as you add more.

Ladle the hot brine into the jars, leaving ½ inch (12 mm) of headspace. Remove any air bubbles and adjust the headspace, if necessary. Wipe the rims clean and seal tightly with the lids.

Process the jars for 10 minutes in a boiling-water bath (for detailed instructions, including cooling and testing seals, see pages 228–229). Let the jars stand undisturbed for 24 hours and then set them aside for 2 weeks for the flavors to develop. The sealed jars can be stored in a cool, dark place for up to 1 year. If a seal has failed, store the jar in the refrigerator for up to 1 week.

3 cups (24 fl oz/750 ml) distilled white vinegar (5 percent acidity)

6 Tbsp (2½ oz/75 g) kosher salt

6 large, mature dill heads, or 6 Tbsp (1½ oz/45 g) dill seeds and 24 fresh dill sprigs

1½ tsp cayenne pepper

6 cloves garlic

4 lb (2 kg) green beans

Makes 6 one-pint (16–fl oz/500-ml) jars

Almost any type of pickled vegetable makes a perfect garnish for a Bloody Mary. Here, Dilly Beans lend a flavorful crunch of dill and vinegar. Add a dash of the brine to the cocktail mixture for extra zing. Omit the vodka to transform this brunch classic into a Virgin Mary.

Spicy Bloody Mary with Dilly Beans

In a pitcher, stir together the tomato juice, vegetable juice cocktail, vodka, lime juice, Worcestershire and Tabasco sauces, and horseradish, if using. Season with salt and pepper. Taste and adjust the seasonings. Refrigerate until ready to serve.

If rimming the glasses with celery salt, pour the salt onto a small plate wider than the rim of the glasses. Moisten the outside edge of each glass rim with a lemon wedge and, holding the rim down at an angle, slowly rotate the edge through the salt.

Fill the glasses three-fourths full with ice cubes. Stir the contents of the pitcher, then pour into the glasses. Garnish with the beans and the lemon wedges, if using.

2½ cups (20 fl oz/625 ml) tomato juice, chilled

2½ cups (20 fl oz/625 ml) vegetable juice cocktail, chilled

1½ cups (12 fl oz/375 ml) vodka

¼ cup (2 fl oz/60 ml) fresh lime juice

2 tsp Worcestershire sauce

½ tsp Tabasco or other hot-pepper sauce, or to taste

1 Tbsp freshly grated horseradish, or to taste (optional)

Salt and freshly ground pepper

3 Tbsp celery salt (optional)

Lemon wedges (optional)

Ice cubes

Dilly Beans (page 135) and/or other pickled vegetables for garnish

Serves 6

Garlic aficionados will be unable to resist these whole cloves accented with lemon and red pepper. Mash the cloves or chop them finely before using them to season a tomato sauce or bean dip. Or, make a sandwich spread with this garlic, some fresh herbs, and mayonnaise.

Pickled Garlic

Have ready hot, sterilized jars and their lids (see page 228).

Working with 1 head of garlic at a time, separate the cloves and peel them, discarding any very small or discolored cloves. Using a cocktail citrus zester, remove long, thin curls of zest from the lemons. (If desired, squeeze the juice from the lemons and reserve for another use.)

In a large nonreactive saucepan, combine the vinegar, lemon juice, and salt. Add 3 cups (24 fl oz/750 ml) water and bring to a boil over medium-high heat, stirring to dissolve the salt.

Divide the lemon zest curls among the jars. In each jar, place 1 tsp red pepper flakes. Fill the jars with the peeled garlic cloves to within ¾ inch (2 cm) of the rims.

Ladle the hot brine into the jars, leaving ½ inch (12 mm) of headspace. Remove any air bubbles and adjust the headspace, if necessary. Wipe the rims clean and seal tightly with the lids.

Process the jars for 3 minutes in a boiling-water bath (for detailed instructions, including cooling and testing seals, see pages 228–229). Let the jars stand undisturbed for 24 hours, and then store in the refrigerator for up to 2 weeks.

20 heads garlic

6 lemons

3 cups (24 fl oz/750 ml) white wine vinegar (6 percent acidity)

2 Tbsp fresh lemon juice

1 Tbsp plus 1 tsp kosher salt

2 Tbsp red pepper flakes

Makes 6 half-pint (8–fl oz/250-ml) jars

These tiny white globes look so beautiful in the jar, you may not want to open it. But once you do and bite into your first onion, you'll want to use the onions not only in classic cocktails but also in salads, on antipasto platters, and as an accompaniment to slices of sharp cheese.

Pickled Cocktail Onions

Have ready hot, sterilized jars and their lids (see page 228).

Blanch and peel the onions (see page 234).

In a large nonreactive saucepan, combine the vinegar and salt. Add 2 cups (16 fl oz/500 ml) water and bring to a boil over medium-high heat, stirring to dissolve the salt.

Meanwhile, in each jar, place 1 bay leaf, 1 tsp mustard seeds, and 1 tsp peppercorns. Pack the jars with the peeled onions to within ¾ inch (2 cm) of the rims.

Ladle the hot brine into the jars, leaving ½ inch (12 mm) of headspace. Remove any air bubbles and adjust the headspace, if necessary. Wipe the rims clean and seal tightly with the lids.

Process the jars for 7 minutes in a boiling-water bath (for detailed instructions, including cooling and testing seals, see pages 228–229). Let the jars stand undisturbed for 12 hours and then set them aside for 2 weeks for the flavors to develop. The sealed jars can be stored in a cool, dark place for up to 1 year. If a seal has failed, store the jar in the refrigerator for up to 1 week.

1½ lb (750 g) pearl onions

2 cups (16 fl oz/500 ml) malt vinegar (5 percent acidity)

1 Tbsp plus 1 tsp kosher salt

6 bay leaves

2 Tbsp mustard seeds

2 Tbsp peppercorns

Makes 6 half-pint (8-fl oz/250-ml) jars

Re-creating deli-style pickled artichoke hearts at home is surprisingly easy, and their texture and flavor are superior to store-bought. Don't be put off by the need to trim the artichokes. Once you prepare the first few, the rest of the batch will go quickly.

Marinated Artichoke Hearts

Have ready hot, sterilized jars and their lids (see page 228).

Half fill a large bowl with water and add the juice of 2 lemons. Working with 1 artichoke at a time, snap off the outer leaves until you reach the tender inner leaves. Cut off the top ½ inch (12 mm), then cut off the stem and trim any dark green skin from the base. Cut the artichoke into quarters, cut away any visible choke, and place in the lemon water.

Using a slotted spoon, transfer the artichokes to a large nonreactive saucepan over medium heat. Add ¼ cup (2 fl oz/60 ml) of the lemon water. Cover and cook, stirring occasionally, until barely tender, about 10 minutes. Return to the bowl of lemon water and stir in the ice cubes.

Meanwhile, in a large nonreactive saucepan, combine the 6 Tbsp lemon juice, the vinegar, and the salt. Add 1½ cups (12 fl oz/375 ml) water and bring to a boil over medium-high heat, stirring to dissolve the salt.

Divide the lemon zest and garlic evenly among the jars, then add a pinch of red pepper flakes, ½ tsp fines herbes, and ¼ tsp peppercorns to each jar. Pack the artichokes tightly into the jars to within 1 inch (2.5 cm) of the rims.

Ladle the hot brine into the jars, leaving ¾ inch (2 cm) of headspace. Add 2 Tbsp olive oil to each jar, leaving ¼–½ inch (6–12 mm) of headspace. Remove any air bubbles and adjust the headspace, if necessary. Wipe the rims and seal tightly with the lids. Let the jars stand undisturbed for 24 hours, and then refrigerate for up to 2 weeks, shaking the jars gently for the first week to mix the flavors.

Juice of 2 lemons, plus 6 Tbsp (3 fl oz/90 ml)

5 lb (2.5 kg) baby artichokes

12–14 ice cubes

1½ cups (12 fl oz/375 ml) white wine vinegar (6 percent acidity)

1 Tbsp plus 1 tsp kosher salt

Long, thin curls of zest from 4 lemons, removed with a cocktail citrus zester

6 cloves garlic, thinly sliced

6 pinches red pepper flakes

1 Tbsp fines herbes

1½ tsp peppercorns

¾ cup (6 fl oz/180 ml) extra-virgin olive oil

Makes 6 half-pint (8-fl oz/250-ml) jars

These homemade cornichons, infused with fresh tarragon and green peppercorns, are nothing like their store-bought counterparts. Look for small pickling cucumbers at farmers' markets, or grow them yourself. Pair with pâté and a baguette for a simple picnic.

Cornichons

Have ready hot, sterilized jars and their lids (see page 228).

In a large nonreactive saucepan, combine the vinegar and salt. Add 2 cups (16 fl oz/500 ml) water and bring to a boil over medium-high heat, stirring to dissolve the salt.

Meanwhile, in each jar, place 2 tarragon sprigs, 1 tsp peppercorns, and 1 tsp mustard seeds. Pack the cucumbers into the jars to within ¾ inch (2 cm) of the rims.

Ladle the hot brine into the jars, leaving ½ inch (12 mm) of headspace. Remove any air bubbles and adjust the headspace, if necessary. Wipe the rims clean and seal tightly with the lids.

Process the jars for 7 minutes in a boiling-water bath (for detailed instructions, including cooling and testing seals, see pages 228–229). Let the jars stand undisturbed for 24 hours and then set them aside for 2 weeks for the flavors to develop. The sealed jars can be stored in a cool, dark place for up to 1 year. If a seal has failed, store the jar in the refrigerator for up to 1 week.

2 cups (16 fl oz/500 ml) white wine vinegar (6 percent acidity)

1 Tbsp plus 1 tsp kosher salt

12 fresh tarragon sprigs

2 Tbsp green peppercorns

2 Tbsp mustard seeds

1 lb (500 g) cornichons (European gherkins) or miniature pickling cucumbers, about 1½ inches (4 cm) long

Makes 6 half-pint (8–fl oz/250-ml) jars

Shallots and delicately minced cornichons make a delectable tartar sauce. The English have long paired vinegar with fried foods, and this tart, creamy sauce complements fried fish fillets. Use lean, firm-fleshed fish such as sole or cod; serve with French fries and lemon wedges.

Fried Fish Fillets with Tartar Sauce

To make the tartar sauce, in a bowl, combine the mayonnaise, mustard, shallots, cornichons, and vinegar. Whisk to mix well. Season with salt and pepper. Cover and refrigerate until ready to serve.

In a bowl, whisk together the milk and egg until blended. Spread the flour on a plate and season with salt and pepper.

Dip each fish strip in the egg mixture and then into the seasoned flour, gently shaking off the excess. Place on a wire rack and let stand for 10 minutes to set the coating.

Preheat the oven to 275°F (135°C). Place an ovenproof platter in the oven.

Pour oil to a depth of 3 inches (7.5 cm) into a wide saucepan, and heat to 375°F (190°C) on a deep-frying thermometer, or until a small piece of bread turns golden within a few seconds of being dropped into the oil. Working in batches, add the fish and fry, turning occasionally, until golden brown, 3–4 minutes. Using a slotted spoon, transfer to paper towels to drain briefly, and then place on the platter in the oven to keep warm until all the fish is fried.

Serve the fish immediately. Accompany with the tartar sauce and the lemon wedges, if using.

FOR THE TARTAR SAUCE

1 cup (8 fl oz/250 ml) mayonnaise

1 Tbsp Dijon mustard (page 194 or purchased)

2 Tbsp minced shallots

3 Tbsp minced Cornichons (facing page)

2 Tbsp vinegar from Cornichons (facing page)

Salt and ground pepper

1 cup (8 fl oz/250 ml) milk

1 egg, lightly beaten

1 cup (5 oz/155 g) all-purpose (plain) flour

Salt and ground pepper

1½ lb (750 g) firm white fish fillets, cut into strips 2 inches (5 cm) long and 1 inch (2.5 cm) wide

Peanut or corn oil for deep-frying

Lemon wedges for serving (optional)

Serves 4–6

Cooks in the American South have long known that pickled okra is as sublime as condiments get. The key is to use the freshest okra you can find to ensure that the pickled vegetable will be crisp. Roll pickled okra in prosciutto, use as a cocktail garnish, or add to egg salad.

Pickled Okra

Have ready hot, sterilized jars and their lids (see page 228).

In a large nonreactive saucepan, combine the vinegar and salt. Add 3½ cups (28 fl oz/875 ml) water and bring to a boil over medium-high heat, stirring to dissolve the salt.

Meanwhile, in each jar, put 1 tsp mustard seeds, ½ tsp cumin seeds, 1 chile, and 4 garlic cloves. Tightly pack the okra, stems ends up, into the jars to within ¾ inch (2 cm) of the rims.

Ladle the hot brine into the jars, leaving ½ inch (12 mm) of headspace. Remove any air bubbles and adjust the headspace, if necessary. Wipe the rims clean and seal tightly with the lids.

Process the jars for 7 minutes in a boiling-water bath (for detailed instructions, including cooling and testing seals, see pages 228–229). Let the jars stand undisturbed for 24 hours and then set them aside for 2 weeks for the flavors to develop. The sealed jars can be stored in a cool, dark place for up to 1 year. If a seal has failed, store the jar in the refrigerator for up to 1 week.

3½ cups (28 fl oz/ 875 ml) cider vinegar (5 percent acidity)

2 Tbsp plus 1 tsp kosher salt

2 Tbsp mustard seeds

1 Tbsp cumin seeds

6 dried whole chiles

24 cloves garlic

3 lb (1.5 kg) okra, stem ends trimmed

Makes 6 one-pint (16–fl oz/500-ml) jars

Nearly everyone likes a good egg salad sandwich. This egg salad is made special with the addition of pickled okra, though you could use almost any pickled vegetable for an equally delicious result. Plain white toast is a classic partner, but crackers are good alternatives.

Egg Salad with Pickled Okra

Fill a large saucepan three-fourths full with lightly salted water and bring to a boil over high heat. Carefully slip the eggs into the water and cover the pan. Reduce the heat to medium and cook for 7–8 minutes. Drain the eggs, transfer to a bowl, and add cold water to cover. When cool enough to handle, peel and chop coarsely.

In a bowl, combine the chopped eggs, okra, shallot, parsley, mustard, paprika, and enough mayonnaise to bind the ingredients. Mix well. Season with salt and pepper. Use immediately, or cover and refrigerate for up to 2 days.

6 eggs, preferably free-range organic

¼ cup (2 oz/60 g) chopped and drained Pickled Okra (page 144)

1 Tbsp finely chopped shallot

1 Tbsp finely chopped fresh flat-leaf (Italian) parsley

1 tsp whole-grain mustard

¼ tsp smoked paprika

3 or 4 Tbsp mayonnaise

Salt and freshly ground pepper

Makes enough for 4 sandwiches

These sour gems are a welcome addition to salads, salsas, and grilled sandwiches. The natural acidity of the green tomatoes paired with the vinegar provides enough acidification that a boiling-water bath is not necessary. Be sure to pour in the brine while it is at a boil.

Pickled Green Tomatoes

Have ready hot, sterilized jars and their lids (see page 228).

In a large nonreactive saucepan, combine the vinegar and salt. Add 4 cups (32 fl oz/1 l) water and bring to a boil over medium-high heat, stirring to dissolve the salt.

Meanwhile, in each jar, place 2 bay leaves, 1 tsp pickling spice, 2 garlic cloves, 1 dill head (or 1 Tbsp dill seeds and 4 dill sprigs), and ⅛ tsp celery seeds. Divide the onion slices among the jars. Pack the tomatoes into the jars to within 1 inch (2.5 cm) of the rims.

Ladle the boiling brine into the jars, leaving ½ inch (12 mm) of headspace. Remove any air bubbles and adjust the headspace, if necessary. Wipe the rims clean and seal tightly with the lids.

Set the jars aside for at least 2 weeks for the flavors to develop. The sealed jars can be stored in a cool, dark place for up to 1 year. If a seal has failed, store the jar in the refrigerator for up to 1 week.

2 cups (16 fl oz/500 ml) cider vinegar (5 percent acidity)

½ cup (4 oz/125 g) kosher salt

12 bay leaves

2 Tbsp pickling spice (page 19 or purchased)

12 cloves garlic

6 large, mature dill heads, or 6 Tbsp (1½ oz/45 g) dill seeds and 24 fresh dill sprigs

¾ tsp celery seeds

1 small yellow onion, cut into slices ¼ inch (6 mm) thick

6 cups (2¼ lb/1.1 kg) green cherry tomatoes

Makes 6 one-pint (16–fl oz/500-ml) jars

Pink peppercorns and honey contribute depth of flavor to pickled jalapeños. The chiles are a classic addition to nachos and quesadillas, and can spice up a marinade for grilled meat or poultry. Their contrast of acidity and heat also make them a great garnish for soups.

Pickled Jalapeño Chiles

Have ready hot, sterilized jars and their lids (see page 228).

In a large nonreactive saucepan, combine the vinegar, honey, and salt and bring to a boil over medium-high heat, stirring to dissolve the salt.

Meanwhile, in each jar, place ½ tsp pickling spice and ½ tsp pink peppercorns. Pack the jars tightly with the jalapeño slices to within ¾ inch (2 cm) of the rims.

Ladle the hot brine into the jars, leaving ½ inch (12 mm) of headspace. Remove any air bubbles and adjust the headspace, if necessary. Wipe the rims clean and seal tightly with the lids.

Process the jars for 7 minutes in a boiling-water bath (for detailed instructions, including cooling and testing seals, see pages 228–229). Let the jars stand undisturbed for 12 hours and then set them aside for 2 weeks for the flavors to develop. The sealed jars can be stored in a cool, dark place for up to 1 year. If a seal has failed, store the jar in the refrigerator for up to 1 week.

4 cups (32 fl oz/1 l) cider vinegar (5 percent acidity)

2 Tbsp honey

1 tsp kosher salt

1 Tbsp pickling spice (page 19 or purchased)

1 Tbsp pink peppercorns

About 20 large or 30 small jalapeño chiles, cut into slices ¼ inch (6 mm) thick

Makes 6 half-pint (8–fl oz/250-ml) jars

Tart lime juice, spicy pickled jalapeños, and creamy avocado all work together to create this well-balanced soup. You can also add 1½ cups (9 oz /280 g) peeled, seeded, and diced tomatoes to the pan when you add the lime juice and cilantro.

Chicken-Lime Soup with Pickled Jalapeños

In a large saucepan over medium heat, warm the olive oil. Add the onion and cook, stirring occasionally, until tender and translucent, about 10 minutes. Add the garlic and cook until softened, 1–2 minutes. Add the broth, raise the heat to high, and bring to a boil.

Reduce the heat to medium-low and add the chicken. Simmer, partially covered, until the chicken is opaque throughout, 10–12 minutes. Using a slotted spoon, transfer the chicken to a cutting board. Reduce the heat to low and keep the soup at a simmer.

When the chicken is cool enough to handle, shred it into bite-sized pieces. Stir the chicken into the soup along with the lime juice and cilantro. Season with salt and pepper, and simmer the soup until the chicken is heated through, about 5 minutes. Taste and adjust the seasoning if needed.

Ladle the soup into warmed bowls. Garnish with the jalapeños, avocado, and tortilla chips, if using. Serve at once.

3 Tbsp olive oil

1 large yellow onion, chopped

2 Tbsp minced garlic

8 cups (64 fl oz/2 l) chicken broth

1¼ lb (625 g) skinless, boneless chicken breasts

6 Tbsp (3 fl oz/90 ml) fresh lime juice

6 Tbsp (½ oz/15 g) chopped fresh cilantro (fresh coriander)

Salt and freshly ground pepper

¼ cup (2 oz/60 g) Pickled Jalapeño Chiles (facing page), or to taste

1 avocado, halved, pitted, peeled, and diced

Crumbled tortilla chips for garnish (optional)

Serves 6

This classic Italian pickle, which makes a great antipasto, contains an array of vegetables preserved to maintain their distinctive flavors and textures. The recipe is flexible: use asparagus or green beans for any of the vegetables, or lemon thyme for the oregano.

Giardiniera

In a large nonreactive bowl, combine the zucchini and celery. Add 1 Tbsp of the salt and the ice cubes. Cover and refrigerate for 2–3 hours. Drain, rinse, and then drain well.

Have ready hot, sterilized jars and their lids (see page 228).

In a large nonreactive saucepan, combine the vinegar and the remaining 1 Tbsp salt. Add 3 cups (24 fl oz/750 ml) water and bring to a boil over medium-high heat, stirring to dissolve the salt.

Meanwhile, cut each bell pepper half into 4 rectangles. Cut the carrots into sticks about ¼ inch (6 mm) thick and at least ½ inch (12 mm) shorter than the height of the jars.

In each jar, place 1 oregano sprig, 3 garlic cloves, 1 bay leaf, and ½ tsp peppercorns. Divide the vegetables among the jars, filling them to within 1 inch (2.5 cm) of the rims.

Ladle the hot brine into the jars, leaving ½ inch (12 mm) of headspace and adding more vinegar if needed. Remove any air bubbles and adjust the headspace, if necessary. Add 1 Tbsp olive oil to each jar. Wipe the rims clean and seal tightly with the lids.

Process the jars for 10 minutes in a boiling-water bath (for detailed instructions, including cooling and testing seals, see pages 228–229). Let the jars stand undisturbed for 24 hours and then set them aside for 2 weeks for the flavors to develop. The sealed jars can be stored in a cool, dark place for up to 1 year. If a seal has failed, store the jar in the refrigerator for up to 1 week.

4 small zucchini (courgettes), about ¾ lb (375 g), cut into rounds ¼ inch (6 mm) thick

10–12 celery stalks, cut on the diagonal into 1-inch (2.5-cm) pieces

2 Tbsp kosher salt

6 ice cubes

3 cups (24 fl oz/750 ml) white wine vinegar (6 percent acidity)

4 red bell peppers (capsicums), about 1½ lb (750 g), halved and seeded

3 or 4 carrots, peeled

6 fresh oregano sprigs

18 cloves garlic

6 bay leaves

1 Tbsp peppercorns

1 small head cauliflower, cut into small florets

6 Tbsp (3 fl oz/90 ml) extra-virgin olive oil

Makes 6 one-pint (16–fl oz/500-ml) jars

Take advantage of olives and pickled vegetables on sandwiches, from tapenade spreads to pickle-studded tuna salad. The muffuletta is a New Orleans classic. Traditionally a round loaf conceals piles of cured meats and cheeses and a salad of olives and pickled vegetables.

Muffuletta Sandwiches

To make the olive salad, in a bowl, stir together the Giardiniera, olives, and red pepper flakes.

Place the rolls, cut sides down, on a work surface and brush the crust sides with the olive oil. Turn the rolls and cover the bottom halves with the salad, dividing it evenly. Layer the salami, provolone, *capocollo*, and mortadella, if using, evenly on top of the salad. Cover with the top halves of the rolls, cut sides down, and press down gently to compact the sandwiches.

Preheat a sandwich grill or the broiler (grill). Place a sandwich in the grill, close the top plate, and cook until the bread is golden, the meats are warmed, and the cheese is nearly melted, 3–5 minutes. Repeat with the remaining 3 sandwiches. Alternatively, place the sandwiches on a baking sheet and broil (grill) until the bread is golden and the cheese is nearly melted, 2–3 minutes.

Transfer the sandwiches to a cutting board, cut each sandwich into quarters, and arrange on individual plates. Serve at once.

FOR THE OLIVE SALAD

1 cup (4 oz/125 g) Giardiniera (page 151), chopped

½ cup (2 oz/60 g) Citrus-Herb Olives (page 134) or other green olives, pitted and chopped

¼ cup (1½ oz/45 g) Kalamata or other black olives, pitted and chopped

⅛ tsp red pepper flakes

4 round Italian rolls, split

2 Tbsp olive oil

¼ lb (125 g) Genoa salami, thinly sliced

4 slices provolone cheese

¼ lb (125 g) *capocollo* or Italian ham, thinly sliced

¼ lb (125 g) mortadella, thinly sliced (optional)

Makes 4 sandwiches

Aromatic tarragon and pleasantly sharp-tasting shallots are an ideal match for the assertive flavor of Brussels sprouts. The pickled sprouts make a wonderful snack. Put out a bowl of them at cocktail hour, and they are guaranteed to heighten the appetites of your dinner guests.

Pickled Brussels Sprouts

Have ready hot, sterilized jars and their lids (see page 228).

Bring a large saucepan of water to a boil over high heat. Have ready a bowl of ice water. Trim ¼ inch (6 mm) from the stem end of each Brussels sprout. Remove and discard the outer leaves. Add the Brussels sprouts to the boiling water and blanch for 1 minute. Using a slotted spoon, transfer to the ice water to cool. Drain well.

In a large nonreactive saucepan, combine the vinegar and salt. Add 3 cups (24 fl oz/750 ml) water and bring to a boil over medium-high heat, stirring to dissolve the salt.

Meanwhile, divide the shallots among the jars, and place 3 tarragon sprigs in each jar. Pack the jars tightly with the Brussels sprouts to within 1 inch (2.5 cm) of the rims.

Ladle the hot brine into the jars, leaving ½ inch (12 mm) of headspace. Remove any air bubbles and adjust the headspace, if necessary. Wipe the rims clean and seal tightly with the lids.

Process the jars for 10 minutes in a boiling-water bath (for detailed instructions, including cooling and testing seals, see pages 228–229). Let the jars stand undisturbed for 12 hours and then set them aside for 2 weeks for the flavors to develop. The sealed jars can be stored in a cool, dark place for up to 1 year. If a seal has failed, store the jar in the refrigerator for up to 1 week.

3½ lb (1.75 kg) Brussels sprouts

3 cups (24 fl oz/750 ml) white wine vinegar (6 percent acidity)

2 Tbsp plus 1 tsp kosher salt

2 shallots, finely chopped

18 fresh tarragon sprigs

Makes 6 one-pint (16–fl oz/500-ml) jars

Spicy Pickled Brussels Sprouts
For spicy sprouts, add 1 or 2 habanero slices, each ¼ inch (6 mm) thick, to each jar.

Roasted bell peppers pickled with fresh garlic and ginger are a pantry staple to keep on hand for numerous uses. Layer the peppers with fresh mozzarella or feta for an appetizer, add them to sandwiches, or cut them into strips and stir them into scrambled eggs or pasta salads.

Pickled Roasted Red Peppers with Garlic

Position a rack in the upper third of the oven and preheat to 450°F (230°C). Place a colander in a large bowl. Line 2 rimmed baking sheets with aluminum foil and top with the peppers. Roast, turning as needed, until evenly charred and blistered, 25–30 minutes. Transfer to the colander, cover, and let stand for 3 hours.

Have ready hot, sterilized jars and their lids (see page 228).

Working over the colander, peel and seed the peppers, capturing the juice in the bowl and placing the cleaned peppers in a second colander over a bowl. Cut the peppers into long strips 2 inches (5 cm) wide. Measure 3 packed cups (30 oz/940 g); reserve the remainder for another use. In a bowl, mix the peppers, ginger, and garlic. Measure the juice from both bowls; you should have about 1½ cups (12 fl oz/375 ml). Pour into a large nonreactive saucepan, and add twice the amount of vinegar. Stir in the sugar and salt and bring to a boil over medium-high heat.

Divide the peppers evenly among the jars. Ladle the hot brine into the jars, leaving ½ inch (12 mm) of headspace. Remove any air bubbles and adjust the headspace, if necessary. Wipe the rims clean and seal tightly with the lids.

Process the jars for 10 minutes in a boiling-water bath (for detailed instructions, including cooling and testing seals, see pages 228–229). Let the jars stand undisturbed for 24 hours and then set them aside for 2 weeks for the flavors to develop. The sealed jars can be stored in a cool, dark place for up to 1 year. If a seal has failed, store the jar in the refrigerator for up to 1 week.

6 lb (3 kg) red bell peppers (capsicums)

¼ cup (2 oz/60 g) peeled and minced fresh ginger

6 cloves garlic, minced

3 cups (24 fl oz/750 ml) distilled white vinegar (5 percent acidity), or as needed

1½ Tbsp sugar

2¼ tsp kosher salt

Makes 6 half-pint (8–fl oz/250-ml) jars

Habanero chiles and a generous quantity of garlic spice up the red onions. It's a good idea to wear rubber gloves when working with chiles, especially habaneros, one of the hotter varieties. The onions complement tacos and are equally delicious on steak or chicken sandwiches.

Mexican-Style Pickled Red Onions

Have ready hot, sterilized jars and their lids (see page 228).

Put the onion slices in a large nonreactive saucepan and add water to cover and 2 tsp of the salt. Bring to a boil over medium-high heat and cook for 1 minute. Drain and return to the pan.

In a mortar and using a pestle, grind the peppercorns and cumin seeds. Add to the pan along with the oregano, garlic, vinegar, lime juice, and remaining 1½ tsp salt. Add 2 cups (16 fl oz/500 ml) water, bring to a boil over medium heat, and simmer for 3 minutes, stirring to dissolve the salt. Remove from the heat.

Select 6 of the most attractive habanero slices that have their seeds attached (reserve the remaining slices for another use). Place 1 slice in the bottom of each jar. Using a slotted spoon, divide the onion slices among the jars, filling them to within ¾ inch (2 cm) of the rims.

Ladle the hot brine into the jars, leaving ½ inch (12 mm) of headspace. Remove any air bubbles and adjust the headspace, if necessary. Wipe the rims clean and seal tightly with the lids. Let the jars stand undisturbed for 24 hours, then store in the refrigerator for up to 2 weeks.

2 lb (1 kg) red onions, cut into slices about ⅛ inch (3 mm) thick

3½ tsp kosher salt

1½ tsp peppercorns

1½ tsp cumin seeds

1 Tbsp dried oregano, preferably Mexican

12 cloves garlic, halved lengthwise

2 cups (16 fl oz/500 ml) cider vinegar (5 percent acidity)

¼ cup (2 fl oz/60 ml) fresh lime juice

3 habanero chiles, cut into slices ¼ inch (6 mm) thick

Makes 6 half-pint (8–fl oz/250-ml) jars

Any firm-fleshed fish can be used to make these addictive tacos. Serve the toppings in small bowls at the table so that diners can choose their own. Don't forget to put out a bowl of salsa—Tomatillo Salsa (page 166) and Mango–Lime Salsa (page 167) are good options.

Fish Tacos with Pickled Onions & Jalapeños

To make a marinade, in a food processor, combine the onion, garlic, serrano chiles, cilantro, and lime juice. Process until a coarse purée forms. Season with salt. Transfer the marinade to a bowl.

Cut the fish fillets into cubes. Add the cubes to the marinade and turn to coat. Cover and marinate at room temperature for 2 hours or in the refrigerator for up to 4 hours.

Remove the fish from the marinade, scraping off the excess. Discard the marinade. Season the fish with salt and pepper.

In a large frying pan over medium-high heat, warm 3 Tbsp olive oil. Add half of the fish and cook, turning once, until well seared, 1–2 minutes on each side. Transfer to a plate. Repeat with the remaining fish, using the remaining 1 Tbsp oil if needed. Break the cubes of cooked fish into smaller pieces.

Place 2 Tbsp of the cabbage in the center of each tortilla. Divide the fish evenly among the tortillas. Add 2–3 jalapeño slices and a few pickled onion slices to each taco. Serve at once with the lime wedges and salsa.

1 onion, cut into chunks

2 cloves garlic

2 serrano chiles, seeded

½ bunch fresh cilantro (fresh coriander), chopped

½ cup (4 fl oz/125 ml) fresh lime juice

Salt and ground pepper

1½ lb (750 g) cod or red snapper fillets

3–4 Tbsp olive oil

1½ cups (4½ oz/140 g) shredded green cabbage

12 corn tortillas, heated

24–36 Pickled Jalapeño Chiles (page 148)

About ½ cup (4 oz/125 g) Mexican-Style Pickled Red Onions (facing page)

Lime wedges and salsa for serving

Serves 6

Bright and bracing, pickled fennel can be enjoyed just a day after it is canned. The orange zest and juice and the mirin highlight the vegetable's sweet anise flavor. The fronds look attractive in the jars and on a serving plate alongside the fennel slices. Pair with fresh goat cheese.

Pickled Fennel with Orange Zest

Have ready hot, sterilized jars and their lids (see page 228).

Cut off the fennel stalks just above the bulbs. Set aside 12 of the most attractive fronds; discard the remaining fronds or reserve for another use. Trim the base of each bulb and remove the outer layer if bruised. Cut the bulbs in half lengthwise. Remove the outermost layer of each half and cut into strips about ¾ inch (2 cm) wide. Cut the rest of the bulb lengthwise into slices ¾ inch thick.

In a large nonreactive saucepan, combine the vinegar, orange juice, and mirin. Bring to a boil over medium-high heat, then immediately remove from the heat.

In a mortar, using a pestle, crush ½ Tbsp of the peppercorns. Divide the crushed pepper evenly among the jars.

Place several fennel strips in each jar. Arrange a fennel frond against the glass for visual effect. Pack the jars with the fennel slices, the orange zest curls, and the remaining fronds, alternating them, to within ¾ inch (2 cm) of the rims. Place ½ tsp of the remaining peppercorns in each jar.

Ladle the vinegar mixture into the jars, leaving ½ inch (12 mm) of headspace. Remove any air bubbles and adjust the headspace, if necessary. Add 1 Tbsp olive oil to each jar. Wipe the rims clean and seal tightly with the lids. Let the jars stand undisturbed for 24 hours, then store in the refrigerator for up to 2 weeks.

4 large fennel bulbs with leaves attached, about 1 lb (500 g) each

1½ cups (12 fl oz/375 ml) white wine vinegar (6 percent acidity)

1½ cups (12 fl oz/375 ml) fresh orange juice (from 3 or 4 navel oranges)

¼ cup (2 fl oz/60 ml) mirin

1 Tbsp pink peppercorns

Long, thin curls zest from 1 navel orange, removed with a cocktail citrus zester (about 3 tsp)

3 Tbsp olive oil

Makes 3 one-pint (16–fl oz/500-ml) jars

Here's a classic way to pickle cabbage and make sauerkraut, known for its puckery flavor. The fermentation process can take several weeks, so don't be impatient. Use a mandoline, a food processor, or a chef's knife to cut the cabbage into thin shreds.

Sauerkraut

Place the cabbage in a large bowl, sprinkle with the 3 Tbsp salt, and toss to combine. Cover and let stand until softened, about 30 minutes.

Working in batches, tightly pack the cabbage into a 4-qt (4-l) ceramic crock or food-grade plastic tub. Add any accumulated liquid from the bowl. Cover the cabbage with cheesecloth (muslin), set a plate on the cloth, and top with heavy weights. Cover the crock with a kitchen towel and let stand at room temperature. Within 24 hours, the cabbage should be submerged in brine. If it isn't, stir 1 tsp salt into 1 cup (8 fl oz/250 ml) water and add to the crock. Check the cabbage every day or two. If scum forms, scrape it off and rinse the plate before returning it. Depending on the temperature, the cabbage will ferment in 10 days to 4 weeks. It is ready when bubbles no longer appear and the aroma is pleasantly pungent, usually about 2 weeks. Taste, and if it is too mild, let it continue to ferment.

Sauerkraut fermentation is an evolutionary process. The flavor will become more concentrated as the weeks go by. Using tongs or a large spoon, remove a serving or a jarful at a time and recover the crock. If you remove more than you can use at one time, refrigerate the remainder in a separate container. Conditions can vary from batch to batch, depending on how cool the storage environment is, but after several weeks the sauerkraut will lose texture and be less tasty. Try to work through your crock in four weeks.

5 lb (2.5 kg) red or green cabbage, or a mixture (about 4 medium heads), tough outer leaves removed, quartered, cored, and finely shredded

3 Tbsp kosher salt, plus extra if needed

Makes 8 one-pint (16–fl oz/500-ml) jars

Flavored Sauerkraut
Mix 3 Tbsp caraway seeds with the cabbage before fermentation. Or, for a colorful variation, add 1 cup (5 oz/155 g) peeled and shredded carrots to the kraut before you pack it into jars.

A Reuben sandwich is all about the quality of ingredients you put into it: use extra-fresh bread, good corned beef and Swiss cheese, and homemade Russian dressing and sauerkraut. Pumpernickel bread can be substituted for the rye, and smoked turkey for the corned beef.

Reuben Sandwiches

To make the dressing, in a small bowl, stir together the mayonnaise, ketchup, onion, and pickle relish until well mixed.

Lay the bread slices on a work surface and spread one side of each slice with the butter. Turn the slices and spread evenly with the dressing.

Sprinkle a bit of cheese on 4 of the dressing-covered slices and top with the meat slices, dividing them evenly. Make sure the meat does not hang over the edges; trim it if necessary. Spread the sauerkraut evenly over the meat, and then distribute the remaining cheese evenly over the sauerkraut. Top with the remaining bread slices, buttered sides out, and press down firmly to compact the sandwiches.

Preheat a sandwich grill. Place a sandwich in the grill, close the top plate, and cook until the bread is golden, 4–5 minutes. Repeat with the remaining 3 sandwiches. Alternatively, heat a large nonstick frying pan over medium-high heat. Place the sandwiches in the hot pan and cook, occasionally pressing down gently on each sandwich with a spatula, until the undersides are golden, 4–5 minutes. Turn the sandwiches and cook, again pressing down on them, until the second sides are golden and the cheese is melted, 3–4 minutes longer.

Transfer the sandwiches to individual plates and serve at once.

FOR THE DRESSING

½ cup (4 fl oz/125 ml) mayonnaise

4 tsp Classic Ketchup (page 192 or purchased)

1 tsp minced yellow onion

1½ Tbsp Sweet Pickle Relish (page 174 or purchased)

8 slices rye bread

¼ cup (2 oz/60 g) unsalted butter, at room temperature

½ lb (250 g) Swiss or Jarlsburg cheese, grated

¼ lb (125 g) sliced corned beef or smoked turkey

1 cup (6 oz/185 g) well-drained Sauerkraut (facing page)

Makes 4 sandwiches

SALSAS, RELISHES & CHUTNEYS

"Toppings like salsas and relishes are a way to create a unique flavor palate, sweet or savory, by combining your favorite fruits and vegetables with different herbs. They remind me of mixing a good cocktail."

LISA ATWOOD

TOMATILLOS • CORN • MANGO • EGGPLANT • ZUCCHINI • CRANBERRIES

Unlike many of their preserving pantry kin, salsas, relishes, and chutneys are chunky rather than smooth. They invariably burst with bright tastes and colors, thanks to the combination of robust flavors and textures, such as tomato and garlic, ginger and cranberry, rhubarb and mint.

Fresh tasting and zingy, salsas typically combine coarsely chopped produce with herbs. Look beyond the familiar tomato base to corn, tomatillos, peppers (capsicums), or nectarines paired with basil, parsley, or mint. To give them an appealing charred flavor, roast or grill the vegetables or fruits beforehand. Serve as dips or toppings for countless dishes.

Relishes, like salsas, are made from diced produce—onions, cucumbers, tomatoes, eggplant, cranberries—but are generally pickled in vinegar. They, too, are versatile, adding zesty flavor to cheese plates, steaks, and sandwiches.

Coarse and highly seasoned, chutneys marry chopped or crushed fruits, such as mangoes, apples, or pears, with spices like star anise, ginger, and cinnamon. Sweet or spicy hot, all are delicious served with everything from bread and cheese to meats and eggs.

This traditional green salsa is fairly mild. If you prefer more heat, leave the seeds and ribs in the jalapeños and/or add another jalapeño or a spicier serrano chile. For a mellower flavor, broil (grill) the tomatillos and chiles until lightly and evenly charred, then peel before using.

Tomatillo Salsa

Have ready hot, clean jars and their lids (see page 228).

Place the tomatillos and the chiles in a blender or food processor and process until chunky. Add the green onions, cilantro, lemon juice, garlic, oregano if using, and salt and pepper. Purée until no large chunks remain, about 2 minutes.

Pour the tomatillo mixture into a large nonreactive saucepan. Bring to a boil over high heat, reduce the heat to medium-low, and simmer, uncovered, stirring occasionally, for 20 minutes. Taste and adjust the seasoning if necessary.

Ladle the hot salsa into the jars, leaving ¼ inch (6 mm) of headspace. Remove any air bubbles and adjust the headspace, if necessary. Wipe the rims clean and seal tightly with the lids.

Process the jars for 15 minutes in a boiling-water bath (for detailed instructions, including cooling and testing seals, see pages 228–229). The sealed jars can be stored in a cool, dark place for up to 1 year. If a seal has failed, store the jar in the refrigerator for up to 2 weeks.

2½ lb (1.25 kg) tomatillos, husks removed and rinsed

1 Anaheim chile, seeded if desired

4 jalapeño chiles, seeded if desired

18 green (spring) onions, white and pale green parts, coarsely chopped (about 1½ cups/ 4½ oz/140 g)

1 cup (1½ oz/45 g) coarsely chopped fresh cilantro (fresh coriander)

6 Tbsp (3 fl oz/90 ml) fresh lemon juice

3 cloves garlic

1 Tbsp chopped fresh oregano (optional)

1½ tsp salt

½ tsp freshly ground pepper

Makes 6 half-pint (8–fl oz/250-ml) jars

Green mangoes may cause a skin irritation on some people. To avoid any reaction, wear rubber gloves when handling them and wash well after any contact. Spoon generous dollops of this tropical salsa over grilled fish, seared ahi tuna, or even a cheese quesadilla.

Mango-Lime Salsa

Have ready hot, sterilized jars and their lids (see page 228).

Peel each mango. Stand it on a narrow edge, then cut down the length of the mango about 1 inch (2.5 cm) to one side of the stem and just grazing the pit. Repeat on the other side of the pit. Cut the mango halves into ½-inch (12-mm) dice and transfer to a large saucepan.

Add the lime juice, sugar, red onion, bell pepper, chiles, garlic, cilantro, and ¼ cup (2 fl oz/60 ml) water to the pan with the mangoes. Stir to mix well. Bring to a boil over high heat, reduce the heat to medium-low, and simmer, uncovered, stirring, until heated through, about 5 minutes.

Ladle the hot salsa into the jars, leaving ¼ inch (6 mm) of headspace. Remove any air bubbles and adjust the headspace, if necessary. Wipe the rims clean and seal tightly with the lids.

Process the jars for 10 minutes in a boiling-water bath (for detailed instructions, including cooling and testing seals, see pages 228–229). The sealed jars can be stored in a cool, dark place for up to 6 months. If a seal has failed, store the jar in the refrigerator for up to 1 week.

4 green (unripe) mangoes (about 2 lb/1 kg)

1 cup (8 fl oz/250 ml) bottled lime juice

¾ cup (6 oz/185 g) plus 2 Tbsp sugar

1 small red onion, cut into ½-inch (12-mm) dice

1 small red bell pepper (capsicum), halved, seeded, and cut into ½-inch (12-mm) dice

2 jalapeño chiles, seeded and minced

2 cloves garlic, minced

¼ cup (⅓ oz/10 g) chopped fresh cilantro (fresh coriander)

Makes 6 half-pint (8–fl oz/250-ml) jars

Halibut needs nothing more than a brush of olive oil and a sprinkle of salt and pepper when paired with this flavorful salsa. Simple yet elegant, this dish fits the menu for a casual weeknight meal or a stylish dinner party. Serve with baby greens tossed in a light vinaigrette.

Halibut with Mango-Lime Salsa

Preheat the broiler (grill). Alternatively, prepare a charcoal or gas grill for direct grilling over medium-high heat and oil the grill rack.

Lightly brush the fish fillets on both sides with olive oil and season with salt and pepper.

Arrange the fish on a baking sheet and broil (grill), turning once, until opaque throughout, 8–10 minutes for each inch (2.5 cm) of thickness. Alternatively, place the fish on the grill rack. Cover the grill, if desired; covering the grill, with the vents open, will cause the fish to cook faster and take on a smokier taste. If the fish is less than 1 inch thick, leave the grill uncovered to prevent overcooking. Grill the fish, turning once, until opaque throughout, 8–10 minutes for each inch of thickness.

Transfer the fish to warmed individual plates and garnish with a generous spoonful of the salsa. Serve at once.

6 halibut steaks or fillets, 6–8 oz (185–250 g) each

Olive oil for brushing

Salt and freshly ground pepper

About 1 cup (8 fl oz/ 250 ml) Mango-Lime Salsa (page 167)

Serves 6

Plum tomatoes have firm flesh that holds up well during cooking, making them a good choice for this spicy salsa. Other varieties can be substituted, but make sure the tomatoes are not overripe. To tame the heat in this versatile salsa, use only 1 jalapeño chile.

Roasted Tomato-Garlic Salsa

Have ready hot, clean jars and their lids (see page 228).

Preheat the broiler (grill). Combine the tomatoes and chile(s) on a baking sheet. Toss with 2 Tbsp of the olive oil and broil (grill) until lightly and evenly charred, 6–10 minutes. Transfer to a plate and let cool slightly. Halve, core, and seed the tomatoes. Halve and seed the chile(s). Place the chile(s) in a food processor.

Preheat the oven to 425°F (220°C). Combine the onion and garlic on the baking sheet, toss with the remaining 1 Tbsp olive oil, and roast until tender and charred at the edges, 10–12 minutes. Add the onion to the processor, then the garlic, squeezing the cloves from their skins. Process until finely chopped. Add the tomatoes and pulse until finely chopped. Transfer the mixture to a large nonreactive saucepan and stir in the lime juice and salt. Bring to a boil over medium-high heat, reduce the heat to low, and simmer, uncovered, for 15 minutes. Add the cilantro and simmer for 5 minutes.

Ladle the hot salsa into the jars, leaving ¼ inch (6 mm) of headspace. Remove any air bubbles and adjust the headspace, if necessary. Wipe the rims clean and seal tightly with the lids.

Process the jars for 15 minutes in a boiling-water bath (for detailed instructions, including cooling and testing seals, see pages 228–229). The sealed jars can be stored in a cool, dark place for up to 6 months. If a seal has failed, store the jar in the refrigerator for up to 1 week.

3½ lb (1.75 kg) plum (Roma) tomatoes or other firm-fleshed sauce tomatoes

1 or 2 jalapeño chiles

3 Tbsp olive oil

1 large white onion, cut into chunks

10 large cloves garlic, unpeeled

¼ cup (2 fl oz/60 ml) fresh lime juice, or to taste

1 tsp salt

⅓ cup (½ oz/15 g) chopped fresh cilantro (fresh coriander), or to taste

Makes 6 half-pint (8-fl oz/250-ml) jars

This updated version of caponata, the classic Sicilian eggplant antipasto, substitutes Greek Kalamata olives, pine nuts, and plenty of fresh basil for the traditional green olives and celery. Serve it with crisp garlic–rubbed toasts, or spoon it alongside grilled chicken or fish.

Eggplant & Tomato Relish

Arrange the eggplant slices in a single layer on paper towels. Sprinkle both sides with the ¼ cup salt and let the eggplant drain for about 1 hour.

Have ready hot, clean jars and their lids (see page 228).

Blanch, peel, and core the tomatoes (see page 234), then cut them into ¾-inch (2-cm) dice. Rinse the eggplant slices under cold running water and pat dry with paper towels. Cut into ¾-inch dice.

In a large nonreactive saucepan over medium heat, warm 3 Tbsp of the olive oil. Working in batches if necessary, add the eggplant and cook, stirring frequently, until lightly browned, about 10 minutes. Transfer to a plate. Add the remaining 1 Tbsp olive oil and reduce the heat to medium-low. Add the onion and cook, stirring frequently, until tender, about 15 minutes. Add the garlic and cook, stirring, for 2 minutes longer. Stir in the tomatoes, olives, pine nuts, capers, and vinegar. Raise the heat to high and bring to a boil. Reduce the heat to medium-low, gently stir in the eggplant and basil, and simmer until heated through, about 5 minutes. Season with salt and pepper.

Ladle the hot relish into the jars, leaving ¼ inch (6 mm) of headspace. Remove any air bubbles and adjust the headspace, if necessary. Wipe the rims clean and seal tightly with the lids.

Process the jars for 20 minutes in a boiling-water bath (for detailed instructions, including cooling and testing seals, see pages 228–229). The sealed jars can be stored in a cool, dark place for up to 6 months. If a seal has failed, store the jar in the refrigerator for up to 2 weeks.

2 lb (1 kg) globe eggplants (aubergines), cut into slices ¾ inch (2 cm) thick

¼ cup (2 oz/60 g) salt

1¼ lb (625 g) tomatoes

4 Tbsp (2 fl oz/60 ml) olive oil

1 yellow onion, halved and cut into slices ¾ inch (2 cm) thick

2 cloves garlic, minced

⅓ cup (2 oz/60 g) pitted Kalamata olives

3 Tbsp pine nuts, lightly toasted

2 Tbsp capers

½ cup (4 fl oz/125 ml) red wine vinegar

⅓ cup (½ oz/15 g) finely sliced fresh basil

Salt and freshly ground pepper

Makes 6 half-pint (8–fl oz/250-ml) jars

Although this zucchini relish is similar to sweet pickle relish, it has a softer texture and a mellower flavor. The best tool for cutting the zucchini is a julienne peeler, which resembles a vegetable peeler but has serrations. You can also chop the zucchini, rather than julienne it.

Pickled Zucchini Relish

Using a handheld julienne peeler or a mandoline, cut the zucchini lengthwise into thin strips. Cut the strips crosswise into matchsticks. Transfer to a large nonreactive bowl. Add the onion, bell pepper, and salt and toss to combine. Cover and let stand at room temperature for at least 6 hours or up to 1 day.

Have ready hot, sterilized jars and their lids (see page 228).

Drain the zucchini mixture in a large colander. Rinse thoroughly and drain again. Transfer to a large nonreactive saucepan and add the sugar, vinegar, celery seeds, nutmeg, turmeric, pepper, and 1 cup (8 fl oz/ 250 ml) water and stir to combine. Bring to a boil over high heat, reduce the heat to medium-low, and simmer, stirring occasionally, until slightly thickened, 25–30 minutes.

Ladle the hot relish into the jars, leaving ¼ inch (6 mm) of headspace. Remove any air bubbles and adjust the headspace, if necessary. Wipe the rims clean and seal tightly with the lids.

Process the jars for 10 minutes in a boiling-water bath (for detailed instructions, including cooling and testing seals, see pages 228–229). The sealed jars can be stored in a cool, dark place for up to 1 year. If a seal has failed, store the jar in the refrigerator for up to 1 month.

2 lb (1 kg) zucchini (courgettes)

1 large yellow or white onion, diced

1 red bell pepper (capsicum), seeded and diced

2 Tbsp salt

1¼ cups (10 oz/315 g) sugar

1 cup (8 fl oz/250 ml) distilled white vinegar

1 tsp celery seeds

1 tsp freshly grated nutmeg

½ tsp ground turmeric

½ tsp freshly ground pepper

Makes 6 half-pint (8-fl oz/250-ml) jars

If you have a garden overflowing with cucumbers, this classic relish is a good way to use your bumper crop. You can dice the vegetables in a food processor or by hand. If you opt for the food processor, be sure you don't overprocess them or the relish will lose its chunky texture.

Sweet Pickle Relish

In a large nonreactive bowl, combine the cucumbers, onion, and bell peppers. Pour the salt over the cucumber mixture, add enough cold water to cover, and stir gently to mix. Cover and let stand at room temperature for at least 6 hours or up to 1 day.

Have ready hot, sterilized jars and their lids (see page 228).

Drain the cucumber mixture in a colander. Rinse thoroughly and drain again. Transfer to a large nonreactive saucepan and add the sugar, vinegar, and celery and mustard seeds. Place the allspice on a square of cheesecloth (muslin). Bring the corners together and tie securely with kitchen string. Add the cheesecloth bag to the cucumber mixture and stir to mix well. Bring to a boil over medium-high heat, reduce the heat to medium-low, and simmer uncovered, stirring frequently, for 10 minutes. Discard the cheesecloth bag.

Ladle the hot relish into the jars, leaving ¼ inch (6 mm) of headspace. Remove any air bubbles and adjust the headspace, if necessary. Wipe the rims clean and seal tightly with the lids.

Process the jars for 10 minutes in a boiling-water bath (for detailed instructions, including cooling and testing seals, see pages 228–229). The sealed jars can be stored in a cool, dark place for up to 1 year. If a seal has failed, store the jar in the refrigerator for up to 1 month.

2½ lb (1.25 kg) cucumbers, finely diced

1 sweet onion such as Vidalia or Rio Sweet, finely diced

1 yellow bell pepper (capsicum), seeded and finely diced

1 red bell pepper (capsicum), seeded and finely diced

¼ cup (2 oz/60 g) kosher salt

3 cups (1½ lb/750 g) sugar

2 cups (16 fl oz/500 ml) cider vinegar

1 Tbsp celery seeds

1 Tbsp brown mustard seeds

2 tsp whole allspice

Makes 4 one-pint (16–fl oz/500-ml) jars

Tart cranberries, spicy ginger, and sweet apples are combined in this classic relish, perfect for the holiday table but delicious any time of the year. Serve it with roast meat—especially turkey, pork, or duck—or use as a condiment in sandwiches made with leftover roast meat.

Cranberry-Ginger Relish

Have ready hot, sterilized jars and their lids (see page 228).

In a large nonreactive saucepan, combine the vinegar, brown sugar, and ½ cup (4 fl oz/125 ml) water. Bring to a boil over medium heat, stirring until the sugar is dissolved.

Stir in the fresh and dried cranberries, ginger, orange zest and juice, and apples. Bring to a boil and cook, stirring, until the fresh cranberries pop and the mixture thickens, 15–20 minutes. Remove from the heat and stir in the walnuts, if using.

Ladle the hot relish into the jars, leaving ¼ inch (6 mm) of headspace. Remove any air bubbles and adjust the headspace, if necessary. Wipe the rims clean and seal tightly with the lids.

Process the jars for 10 minutes in a boiling-water bath (for detailed instructions, including cooling and testing seals, see pages 228–229). The sealed jars can be stored in a cool, dark place for up to 2 months. If a seal has failed, store the jar in the refrigerator for up to 1 week.

½ cup (4 fl oz/125 ml) cider vinegar

2 cups (14 oz/440 g) firmly packed light brown sugar

3½ cups (14 oz/440 g) fresh cranberries

1 cup (4 oz/125 g) dried cranberries

¼ cup (1½ oz/45 g) crystallized ginger, chopped

2 Tbsp grated orange zest

1 cup (8 fl oz/250 ml) fresh orange juice

1 lb (500 g) Granny Smith apples, peeled, cored, and cut into ¼-inch (6-mm) dice

½ cup (2 oz/60 g) chopped walnuts, toasted (optional)

Makes 5 half-pint (8–fl oz/250-ml) jars

Here is a delectable use for leftover holiday turkey and cranberry relish. For a decadent alternative, substitute Brie cheese for the Cheddar. Or, make cold sandwiches, using two slices of bread for each one and adding a few lettuce leaves and a bit of mustard.

Turkey Melts with Cranberry-Ginger Relish

Preheat the broiler (grill).

Arrange the bread slices on a baking sheet and lightly brush both sides with the olive oil. Broil (grill), turning once, until lightly golden, 30–60 seconds on each side.

Spread the toasted bread with mayonnaise, if using, and then with a generous amount of relish. Top with the turkey slices, distributing them evenly. Sprinkle with the cheese, again dividing evenly.

Return to the broiler and grill until the cheese melts, 30–60 seconds. Transfer to individual plates and serve at once.

6 slices coarse country bread, each about ½ inch (12 mm) thick

2 Tbsp olive oil

Mayonnaise for spreading (optional)

About 1 cup (10 oz/315 g) Cranberry-Ginger Relish (facing page)

1½ lb (750 g) thickly sliced roast turkey

6 oz (185 g) Cheddar cheese, shredded

Serves 6

Bright and colorful, this relish makes good use of late-summer vegetables. To add some fire, stir in 1 or 2 jalapeño or other chiles, finely chopped, with the bell peppers. This versatile condiment goes particularly well with grilled hot dogs, steaks, hamburgers, or chicken.

Corn, Onion & Pepper Relish

Have ready hot, clean jars and their lids (see page 228).

Blanch, peel, and core the tomatoes (see page 234), then halve them and scoop out and discard the seeds. Chop the tomatoes and set aside.

Hold 1 ear of corn upright, stem end down, in a shallow bowl and, using a sharp knife, cut down between the kernels and the cob, rotating the ear after each cut. Repeat with as many ears as necessary until you have 3 cups (18 oz/560 g) corn kernels.

In a large nonreactive saucepan, combine the tomatoes, corn, onions, bell peppers, sugar, mustard seeds, salt, pepper, and cider. Bring to a boil over high heat, reduce the heat to medium-low, and simmer, uncovered, stirring occasionally, until the corn is tender, 10–15 minutes.

Ladle the hot relish into the jars, leaving ¼ inch (6 mm) of headspace. Remove any air bubbles and adjust the headspace, if necessary. Wipe the rims clean and seal tightly with the lids.

Process the jars for 15 minutes in a boiling-water bath (for detailed instructions, including cooling and testing seals, see pages 228–229). The sealed jars can be stored in a cool, dark place for up to 3 months. If a seal has failed, store the jar in the refrigerator for up to 1 week.

2 tomatoes

About 8 ears corn, husks and silk removed

3 red onions, finely chopped

2 green bell peppers (capsicums), seeded and finely chopped

1 red bell pepper (capsicum), seeded and finely chopped

1 orange bell pepper (capsicum), seeded and finely chopped

½ cup (4 oz/125 g) sugar

1 Tbsp mustard seeds

1 Tbsp salt

½ tsp freshly ground pepper

½ cup (4 fl oz/125 ml) sweet apple cider or apple juice

Makes 4 one-pint (16-fl oz/500-ml) jars

Flank steak, a flavorful but not-so-tender cut, benefits from marinating before grilling. Top round, often sold as London broil, or skirt steak can be substituted for the flank steak. Spoon the relish on top of each serving, or pass it in a bowl at the table.

Grilled Steak with Corn, Onion & Pepper Relish

In a bowl, whisk together the orange juice, olive oil, garlic, chili powder, and cumin. Pour half of the marinade into a shallow glass dish. Place the steak in the dish and pour the remaining marinade over the top. Let stand at room temperature for at least 15 minutes, or cover and refrigerate for up to 1 hour.

Prepare a charcoal or gas grill for direct grilling over medium-high heat, and oil the grill rack.

Remove the steak from the marinade, scraping off the excess; discard the marinade. Place the steak on the grill rack and grill, turning once, until done to your liking, about 4 minutes on each side for medium-rare. Transfer to a cutting board and tent loosely with aluminum foil. Let rest for 5 minutes. Cut the steak on the diagonal across the grain into slices about ¼ inch (6 mm) thick.

Arrange the slices on individual plates and serve at once with the relish.

⅓ cup (3 fl oz/80 ml) fresh orange juice

3 Tbsp olive oil

2 cloves garlic, minced

2 tsp chili powder

½ tsp ground cumin

1 flank steak, about 1½ lb (750 g)

Corn, Onion & Pepper Relish (facing page) for serving

Serves 6

Indian cooks typically grind and blend their own spices for the curry powder they use in their chutneys. This simplified chutney calls for commercial curry powder and already-ground spices with good results. If you can't find raw cane sugar, use light brown sugar instead.

Curried Yellow Tomato Chutney

Have ready hot, clean jars and their lids (see page 228).

Blanch, peel, and core the tomatoes (see page 234), then cut them into large chunks. You should have about 10 cups (3¾ lb/1.85 kg).

Cut each onion into quarters through the stem end, and then cut each quarter crosswise into slices, separating the rings. Cut each chile in half lengthwise and remove the stem, seeds, and ribs. Cut each half in half again lengthwise and then thinly slice crosswise.

In a small cup, stir together the curry powder, mustard seeds, cumin, and chili powder. In a large nonreactive saucepan over medium heat, warm the oil. Add the spices and cook, stirring constantly, for 1 minute; do not allow the spices to smoke or burn. Add the chiles, garlic, and ginger and cook, stirring, for 2 minutes longer. Stir in the tomatoes, onions, vinegar, sugar, and ¾ tsp salt.

Bring to a boil over high heat, reduce the heat to medium-low, and simmer, uncovered, stirring occasionally, until the mixture has thickened, about 1 hour. Season with salt and pepper.

Ladle the hot chutney into the jars, leaving ¼ inch (6 mm) of headspace. Remove any air bubbles and adjust the headspace, if necessary. Wipe the rims clean and seal tightly with the lids.

Process the jars for 15 minutes in a boiling-water bath (for detailed instructions, including cooling and testing seals, see pages 228–229). The sealed jars can be stored in a cool, dark place for up to 1 year. If a seal has failed, store the jar in the refrigerator for up to 2 weeks.

5 lb (2.5 kg) yellow tomatoes

2 large yellow onions

2 fresh green chiles such as Anaheim

1 Tbsp plus ½ tsp curry powder

1 tsp brown mustard seeds

1 tsp ground cumin

¾ tsp chili powder

¼ cup (2 fl oz/60 ml) canola oil

4 cloves garlic, grated

2 Tbsp peeled and grated fresh ginger

¾ cup (6 fl oz/180 ml) malt vinegar

½ cup (4 oz/125 g) raw cane sugar (see note)

¾ tsp salt, plus salt to taste

Freshly ground pepper

Makes 7 half-pint (8-fl oz/250-ml) jars

Curried chutney is a fitting accompaniment to these crunchy fritters, although Apple–Onion Chutney (facing page) would work as well. Serve them as a starter for an Indian-inspired meal, or pass them at a cocktail party. The recipe can be easily doubled or tripled.

Spicy Potato Fritters with Chutney

In a bowl, combine the flour, broth, 1 Tbsp peanut oil, garam masala, turmeric, and baking powder. Stir until well mixed. Stir in the green onions, serrano chile, and cilantro. The batter should be thick. Season with salt and pepper.

Pour oil into a large frying pan to a depth of 1 inch (2.5 cm) and heat over medium heat to 350°F (180°C) on a deep-frying thermometer.

Meanwhile, peel and thinly slice the yam and the baking potato.

Working in batches, dip the slices into the batter and then slip them into the hot oil. Fry, turning once, until golden brown on both sides, 3–5 minutes on each side. Using a slotted spoon or tongs, transfer to paper towels to drain.

Transfer to a warmed serving platter and serve at once with the chutney.

1 cup (5½ oz/170 g) chickpea (garbanzo bean) flour

1 cup (8 fl oz/250 ml) vegetable broth or water

1 Tbsp peanut oil, plus more for frying

1 Tbsp garam masala

½ tsp ground turmeric

½ tsp baking powder

2 green (spring) onions, including tender green parts, minced

1 serrano chile, seeded and minced

2 Tbsp minced fresh cilantro (fresh coriander)

Salt and freshly ground pepper

1 yam or sweet potato

1 baking potato

Curried Yellow Tomato Chutney (page 181)

Serves 8

Any apple variety works well in this traditional English chutney, although good baking apples, such as Granny Smith and pippin, that hold their shape when cooked ensure a chunkier result. Serve as an accompaniment to roast pork loin or roast beef.

Apple-Onion Chutney

Have ready hot, sterilized jars and their lids (see page 228).

In a nonreactive saucepan, combine the raisins, vinegar, sugar, zest strips, and cloves. Add 2½ cups (20 fl oz/625 ml) water and stir to mix well. Bring to a boil over high heat. Remove from the heat and set aside.

In a large nonreactive saucepan over medium-low heat, melt the butter with the olive oil. Add the onions and cook, stirring occasionally, until tender, about 15 minutes. Add the raisin mixture and the apples. Bring to a boil over high heat, reduce the heat to medium-low, and simmer, uncovered, stirring occasionally, until the apples are just tender, about 25 minutes. Add the mint and thyme and continue to cook until the apples are tender, about 5 minutes longer. Discard the zest strips.

Ladle the hot chutney into the jars, leaving ¼ inch (6 mm) of headspace and using a small rubber spatula to gently push the apple and onion pieces into the jar so that they are covered with liquid. Remove any air bubbles and adjust the headspace, if necessary. Wipe the rims clean and seal tightly with the lids.

Process the jars for 10 minutes in a boiling-water bath (for detailed instructions, including cooling and testing seals, see pages 228–229). The sealed jars can be stored in a cool, dark place for up to 1 year. If a seal has failed, store the jar in the refrigerator for up to 2 weeks.

2 cups (12 oz/375 g) raisins

1 cup (8 fl oz/250 ml) cider vinegar

1 cup (7 oz/220 g) firmly packed light brown sugar

4 lemon zest strips, each ½ inch (12 mm) wide and 2 inches (5 cm) long

½ tsp ground cloves

2 Tbsp unsalted butter

2 Tbsp olive oil

2 large yellow onions, chopped (about 4 cups/ 1 lb/500 g)

4 lb (2 kg) apples (see note), peeled, cored, and chopped

3 Tbsp chopped fresh mint

1 Tbsp fresh thyme leaves

Makes 4 one-pint (16–fl oz/500-ml) jars

Partnered with a holiday ham or turkey, or with roast pork loin, this beautiful chutney serves as a delicious reminder of summer's bounty. It also makes an elegant addition to a cheese plate and pairs especially well with a creamy St. André or a tangy goat cheese.

Stone-Fruit Chutney

In a large nonreactive saucepan, stir together the vinegar and sugar. Blanch and peel the peaches (see page 234), then halve them and remove the pits. Cut the peach halves into thick slices and add to the pan along with the apricots and cherries. Toss the fruit to coat with the vinegar-sugar mixture. Place the cloves, cardamom pods, peppercorns, and anise seeds on a square of cheesecloth (muslin). Tie the corners together with kitchen string and add to the pan along with the orange zest and cinnamon sticks. Let stand at room temperature for 1 hour.

Have ready hot, clean jars and their lids (see page 228).

Place the pan over medium-high heat and bring to a boil. Reduce the heat to medium-low and simmer, uncovered, stirring occasionally, until thickened and almost jamlike, about 1 hour and 15 minutes. Discard the cloth bag and cinnamon sticks.

Ladle the hot chutney into the jars, leaving ¼ inch (6 mm) of headspace. Remove any air bubbles and adjust the headspace, if necessary. Wipe the rims clean and seal tightly with the lids.

Process the jars for 15 minutes in a boiling-water bath (for detailed instructions, including cooling and testing seals, see pages 228–229). The sealed jars can be stored in a cool, dark place for up to 1 year. If a seal has failed, store the jar in the refrigerator for up to 2 months.

1 cup (8 fl oz/250 ml) golden balsamic vinegar

1½ cups (12 oz/375 g) granulated sugar

2 lb (1 kg) peaches or nectarines

2½ lb (1.25 kg) apricots, plums, or pluots, pitted and sliced

1 lb (500 g) cherries, pitted and halved

2 tsp whole cloves

2 tsp cardamom pods

1½ tsp black peppercorns, crushed

½ tsp anise seeds

4 orange zest strips, each 1 inch (2.5 cm) wide and 2 inches (5 cm) long

2 cinnamon sticks

Makes 7 half-pint (8–fl oz/250-ml) jars

Rhubarb aficionados prize the spring vegetable for its vivid pink hue, its distinctive tartness, and its jamlike texture when cooked. A generous amount of sugar and fresh mint tempers rhubarb's natural acidity. Serve the chutney with grilled lamb chops or roast turkey.

Rhubarb-Mint Chutney

Have ready hot, sterilized jars and their lids (see page 228).

Trim the ends of the rhubarb stalks and cut the stalks lengthwise into quarters, then crosswise into matchstick-size lengths.

Place the cloves on a square of cheesecloth (muslin). Bring the corners together and tie securely with kitchen string. In a large nonreactive saucepan over medium heat, heat the olive oil. Add the cloves, onions, plums, and orange zest and sauté until the onions are tender, about 10 minutes. Add the rhubarb, vinegar, sugar, 1/4 tsp salt, and 1 1/2 tsp pepper and cook, stirring occasionally, until the rhubarb is tender, about 10 minutes. Stir in the mint. Taste and adjust the seasoning.

Ladle the hot chutney into the jars, leaving 1/4 inch (6 mm) of headspace. Remove any air bubbles and adjust the headspace, if necessary. Wipe the rims clean and seal tightly with the lids.

Process the jars for 10 minutes in a boiling-water bath (for detailed instructions, including cooling and testing seals, see pages 228–229). The sealed jars can be stored in a cool, dark place for up to 1 year. If a seal has failed, store the jar in the refrigerator for up to 1 month.

1 1/2 lb (750 g) rhubarb (about 5 large stalks)

1 1/2 tsp whole cloves, lightly crushed

1 Tbsp olive oil

2 yellow onions, coarsely chopped (about 3 1/2 cups/ 14 oz/440 g)

4 red plums (about 1 lb/500 g), pitted and cut into large chunks

1 Tbsp plus 1 tsp minced orange zest

1/2 cup (4 fl oz/125 ml) white wine vinegar

1/4 cup (2 oz/60 g) plus 2 Tbsp sugar

Salt and freshly ground pepper

1/2 cup (1/2 oz/15 g) coarsely chopped fresh mint

Makes 4 half-pint (8-fl oz/250-ml) jars

Bite-sized crostini are the perfect canvas for countless flavor and color combinations. Here, the tart sweetness of rhubarb chutney contrasts with goat cheese and fresh mint for a robust-flavored, visually appealing appetizer. Ricotta cheese can be substituted for the goat cheese.

Crostini with Rhubarb-Mint Chutney

Position a rack in the upper third of the oven and preheat the oven to 450°F (230°C).

Cut the baguette on the diagonal into 24 slices each about ¼ inch (6 mm) thick. Reserve any remaining bread for another use. Arrange the slices on a baking sheet and lightly brush both sides with the 2 Tbsp olive oil. Toast, turning once, until lightly golden, about 2 minutes on each side. Watch carefully and do not allow the crostini to burn or get too hard.

Spread each toast with about 2 tsp of the chutney. Top with a sprinkle of goat cheese and a mint leaf. Drizzle with oil, sprinkle with salt and pepper, and serve at once.

1 baguette

2 Tbsp olive oil, plus more for drizzling

About 1 cup (10 oz/315 g) Rhubarb-Mint Chutney (facing page)

About 1 cup (5 oz/155 g) crumbled goat cheese

24 small fresh mint leaves

Salt and freshly ground pepper

Makes 24 crostini

CONDIMENTS & SAUCES

"Those tomatoes that just keep coming? They're the quintessential ingredient for condiments and sauces, from ketchup to spaghetti sauce studded with basil. Nothing says summer like that fresh tomato flavor."

LISA ATWOOD

TOMATOES • PEACHES • PEPPERS • APPLES • BASIL • BLUEBERRIES

A dish, whether a roasted chicken or a pile of French fries, is typically the star of the show, but a condiment or sauce is a critical supporting player, delivering welcome added flavor. Condiments and sauces can be smooth or slightly chunky—syrups, dressings, or pastes—and are often used as toppings, marinades, or rubs. You can craft them from almost any fresh fruit or vegetable, with tomatoes, peppers (capsicums), apples, berries, and stone fruits among the most popular choices.

Everyone looks for ketchup and mustard on the condiment tray, but pepper sauce and plum sauce belong there, too. Pungent or mild, savory or subtly sweet, these flavorful concoctions complement a wide variety of dishes, from tangy peach barbecue sauce slathered on grilled ribs to applesauce alongside pork chops.

You can also infuse vinegars, oils, and spirits with citrus fruits, herbs, or berries, and then dress up salads and vegetables with the oils and vinegars, or give your favorite cocktail a new flavor with a heady homemade spirit. Or, you can put up sweet and herbaceous infusions, like honey flavored with lavender or lemon verbena, and drizzle them over cheese or muffins.

Make this ketchup when tomatoes are at their summer best. Sweet, juicy garden-fresh tomatoes are reduced to a gently spiced, lusciously thick condiment. Your favorite purchased ketchup will never taste the same after you sample this irresistible homemade version.

Classic Ketchup

Have ready hot, sterilized jars and their lids (see page 228).

Blanch, peel, and core the tomatoes (see page 234), then cut into quarters. In a large nonreactive saucepan over medium-low heat, warm the olive oil. Add the onions and peppers and cook until tender, about 5 minutes. Add the tomatoes and cook until tender, about 30 minutes.

Meanwhile, place the garlic and the spices on a square of cheesecloth (muslin), bring the corners together, and tie with kitchen string. In a small nonreactive saucepan, bring the vinegar and cheesecloth bag to a boil over medium-high heat, cover, and remove from the heat.

Pass the tomato mixture through a food mill into a clean nonreactive saucepan. Discard the cheesecloth bag and pour all but ¼ cup (2 fl oz/ 60 ml) of the vinegar into the tomato mixture. Stir in the sugar and the salt. Bring to a boil over high heat, reduce the heat to medium, and simmer, stirring often, until the mixture is reduced by more than half and mounds slightly on a spoon, 45–60 minutes. Taste and adjust the seasoning with salt, sugar, and the remaining vinegar.

Ladle the hot ketchup into the jars, leaving ¼ inch (6 mm) of headspace. Remove any air bubbles and adjust the headspace, if necessary. Wipe the rims clean and seal tightly with the lids.

Process the jars for 10 minutes in a boiling-water bath (for detailed instructions, including cooling and testing seals, see pages 228–229). The sealed jars can be stored in a cool, dark place for up to 1 year. If a seal has failed, store the jar in the refrigerator for up to 1 month.

12 lb (6 kg) tomatoes

1 Tbsp olive oil

3 yellow onions, coarsely chopped

3 small red bell peppers (capsicums), seeded and coarsely chopped

4 cloves garlic, lightly crushed

1 cinnamon stick, crushed

1 Tbsp celery seeds

1½ tsp whole allspice

1½ tsp whole cloves

½ tsp peppercorns

½ tsp red pepper flakes

1½ cups (12 fl oz/375 ml) cider vinegar

2 Tbsp sugar

1½ tsp salt

Makes 6 half-pint (8–fl oz/250-ml) jars

Pairing chipotle chiles and tomatoes yields a perfectly balanced accompaniment especially suited to grilled meats such as hamburger, flank or skirt steak, or pork chops. The chiles, jalapeños that have been dried in a smoke-filled chamber, have a deep, sweet flavor.

Chipotle Ketchup

Have ready hot, clean jars and their lids (see page 228).

Blanch, peel, and core the tomatoes (see page 234), then cut into chunks. In a large nonreactive saucepan over medium heat, warm the olive oil. Add the onions and cook until translucent, about 5 minutes. Add the garlic, coriander, and allspice and cook until fragrant, about 2 minutes longer. Add the tomatoes, vinegar, and sugar and cook, uncovered, stirring occasionally, until the tomatoes are tender, about 30 minutes.

Meanwhile, cut the chiles in half and remove some or all of the seeds, depending on how spicy you want the ketchup. Reserve the adobo sauce and chop the chiles. When the tomatoes are ready, stir in the chiles and ¼ cup (2 fl oz/60 ml) of the sauce. Let cool briefly.

Working in batches, transfer the tomato mixture to a blender and purée until smooth. Return the puréed mixture to the pan and bring to a boil over high heat. Reduce the heat to medium-low and simmer, stirring often, until thickened, about 20 minutes. Season with salt.

Ladle the hot ketchup into the jars, leaving ¼ inch (6 mm) of headspace. Remove any air bubbles and adjust the headspace, if necessary. Wipe the rims clean and seal tightly with the lids.

Process the jars for 15 minutes in a boiling-water bath (for detailed instructions, including cooling and testing seals, see pages 228–229). The sealed jars can be stored in a cool, dark place for up to 1 year. If a seal has failed, store the jar in the refrigerator for up to 1 month.

4 lb (2 kg) tomatoes

2 Tbsp olive oil

2 yellow onions, coarsely chopped

4 cloves garlic, crushed

1 tsp ground coriander

½ tsp ground allspice

½ cup (4 fl oz/125 ml) cider vinegar

⅔ cup (5 oz/155 g) firmly packed light brown sugar

1 can (7 oz/220 g) chipotle chiles in adobo sauce

Salt to taste

Makes 6 half-pint (8–fl oz/250-ml) jars

The famed mustard associated with Dijon, France, is easy to make. Some versions require grinding whole mustard seeds and spices. This one champions simplicity by combining dry mustard with a few essential ingredients. The result is smooth and creamy, and not too hot.

Dijon-Style Mustard

Have ready hot, sterilized jars and their lids (see page 228).

In a bowl, stir together the mustard and ½ cup (4 fl oz/125 ml) water until smooth. Set aside.

In a small nonreactive saucepan, combine the wine, onion, and garlic. Bring to a boil over high heat. Reduce the heat to medium, stir in the sugar and salt, and simmer, uncovered, stirring often, until reduced by half, about 20 minutes.

Pour the wine mixture through a fine-mesh sieve into the mustard and stir until combined. Transfer to the saucepan and cook over medium heat, stirring frequently, until thickened, about 20 minutes.

Spoon the hot mustard into the jars, leaving ¼ inch (6 mm) of headspace. Remove any air bubbles and adjust the headspace, if necessary. Wipe the rims clean and seal tightly with the lids. Store the jars in the refrigerator for up to 1 year. For the best flavor, let the mustard stand for at least 2 weeks before using.

1⅓ cups (4 oz/125 g) dry mustard

2 cups (16 fl oz/500 ml) dry white wine or flat Champagne

1 yellow onion, chopped

3 cloves garlic, finely chopped

2 tsp sugar

2 tsp salt

Makes 2 half-pint (8–fl oz/250-ml) jars

Honey Dijon
Omit the sugar. Stir in 2 Tbsp honey before transferring the mustard to the jars.

Tarragon Dijon
Add 1 Tbsp chopped fresh tarragon before transferring the mustard to the jars.

Dijon with Mustard Seeds
Add 2 tsp brown mustard seeds during the last 5 minutes of cooking.

Bread crumbs are often used in meat loaves to bind ground meat and seasonings into a firm loaf. Here, rolled oats are soaked in milk and then mixed with the meat to produce a loaf with a nutty flavor and creamy texture. Bright and acidic, ketchup is the perfect condiment.

Meat Loaf with Homemade Ketchup

In a small frying pan over medium-high heat, warm the olive oil. Add the onion and cook, stirring, until soft, about 3 minutes. Stir in 1 tsp of the salt and the pepper. Let cool.

Pour the milk into a small saucepan over medium heat and heat until small bubbles appear along the edge of the pan. Pour the milk into a large bowl. Stir in the oats and the remaining 1 tsp salt. Let stand until the liquid is absorbed, about 15 minutes.

Preheat the oven to 350°F (180°C).

Add the onion, egg, and 1 cup ketchup to the oat mixture and stir to incorporate. Fold in the ground meats and mix gently with your hands just until the liquid is evenly distributed. Do not overmix, or the meat loaf will be tough and crumbly.

Pack the meat mixture into an 8½-by-4½-inch (21.5-by-11.5-cm) loaf pan, mounding the top. Place in a baking pan to collect any overflowing juices. Bake the meat loaf for 1 hour. Remove from the oven and pour off the fat. Return to the oven and continue to bake until the juices run clear when the meat loaf is pierced in the center, or an instant-read thermometer inserted into the thickest part registers 165°F (74°C), 30–45 minutes longer. If the top of the loaf is browning too quickly, tent loosely with aluminum foil.

Remove the meat loaf from the oven and let stand for 5 minutes before slicing. Serve at once, passing ketchup at the table.

1 Tbsp olive oil

1 small yellow onion, finely chopped

2 tsp salt

1 tsp freshly ground pepper

½ cup (4 fl oz/125 ml) milk

1 cup (3 oz/90 g) old-fashioned rolled oats

1 egg, beaten

1 cup (8 fl oz/250 ml) Classic Ketchup (page 192), plus more for serving

1½ lb (750 g) ground (minced) pork

1½ lb (750 g) ground (minced) beef round or sirloin

Serves 8–10

These mini hamburgers—reputedly known as "sliders" because they can slide right down your throat—are irresistible to burger connoisseurs of all ages. Set out a plate of these at a party and they will disappear in minutes. Chipotle-infused ketchup adds an extra kick.

Cheddar Sliders with Chipotle Ketchup

Lightly oil a large cast-iron frying pan or griddle and heat over medium heat until hot. Meanwhile, in a bowl, lightly mix together the beef, salt, and pepper. Handling the beef as little as possible, form 8 small, plump patties about 3 inches (7.5 cm) in diameter and 1½ inches (4 cm) thick.

Place the patties in the pan and cook until browned on the undersides, about 3 minutes. Turn the burgers and place a slice of cheese on top of each burger. Add the onion to the pan alongside the burgers and cook until the onions are softened and the burgers are browned on the second sides, 3–4 minutes longer for medium-rare.

Arrange the rolls on individual plates or a platter. Place a burger on the bottom half of each roll and top with the onions. Spread the top half of each roll with ketchup and place on top of the burger. Serve at once.

Canola oil for coating

1¼ lb (625 g) ground (minced) beef round

1 tsp salt

1 tsp freshly ground pepper

8 small slices Cheddar cheese

1 small white or yellow onion, thinly sliced

8 dinner rolls or mini hamburger buns, split

Chipotle Ketchup (page 193) for serving

Serves 4

A classic Italian–style bruschetta calls for grilled bread slices rubbed with garlic, drizzled with extra-virgin olive oil, sprinkled with salt, and topped with diced summer tomatoes and basil. Adding a thin slice of ricotta salata or mozzarella cheese turns this starter into heartier fare.

Tomato Bruschetta

Preheat the broiler (grill). Alternatively, preheat a charcoal or gas grill for direct grilling over medium-high heat, and oil the grill rack.

Arrange the bread slices on a baking sheet or on a grill rack, and broil or grill, turning once, until lightly toasted on both sides, about 2 minutes total. Immediately rub one side of each slice with the cut side of a garlic clove and drizzle with oil.

Arrange the grilled bread, garlic-rubbed side up, on a serving platter. Spoon on the topping, dividing it evenly. Sprinkle with salt. Top with the cheese slices, if using. Serve at once.

8 slices coarse country bread, each about ½ inch (12 mm) thick

2 large cloves garlic, halved

2 Tbsp extra-virgin olive oil

1½ cups (12 fl oz/375 ml) Bruschetta Topping (page 200)

Coarse sea salt

8 thin slices ricotta salata or mozzarella cheese (optional)

Serves 4

The term "bruschetta" refers to the crisp, garlic-rubbed toasts on which this chunky tomato and basil topping is traditionally served (see page 199). Golden balsamic vinegar lends a subtle tang without adding color. Substitute red balsamic if you can't find the golden variety.

Bruschetta Topping

Have ready hot, clean jars and their lids (see page 228).

Blanch, peel, and core the tomatoes (see page 234), then cut them into ¾-inch (2-cm) chunks.

In a large nonreactive saucepan, combine the wine, wine and balsamic vinegars, and garlic. Bring to a boil over high heat and cook until reduced by about one-third, about 5 minutes. Stir in the tomatoes. Reduce the heat to medium and cook uncovered, stirring occasionally, until the tomatoes are hot throughout, about 10 minutes. Stir in the basil and lemon juice. Season with salt and pepper.

Ladle the hot tomatoes into the jars, leaving ¼ inch (6 mm) of headspace. Gently push on the tomatoes with a rubber spatula to cover them with liquid. Add more liquid from the saucepan if needed to cover the tomatoes completely. Remove any air bubbles and adjust the headspace, if necessary. Wipe the rims clean and seal tightly with the lids.

Process the jars for 20 minutes in a boiling-water bath (for detailed instructions, including cooling and testing seals, see pages 228–229). The sealed jars can be stored in a cool, dark place for up to 6 months. If a seal has failed, store the jar in the refrigerator for up to 2 weeks.

5 lb (2.5 kg) tomatoes, preferably plum (Roma)

1¼ cups (10 fl oz/310 ml) dry white wine

2 Tbsp white wine vinegar

2 Tbsp golden balsamic vinegar

4 cloves garlic, minced

⅓ cup (¾ oz/20 g) firmly packed chopped fresh basil

2 Tbsp fresh lemon juice

Salt and freshly ground pepper

Makes 6 half-pint (8–fl oz/250-ml) jars

Combining different bell peppers will work fine in this sauce, but using a single color will give it the most vivid hue. If you choose orange or yellow peppers, you may want to use golden balsamic vinegar. Serve the sauce alongside vegetables, chicken, shellfish, or fish.

Summer Pepper Sauce

Have ready hot, sterilized jars and their lids (see page 228).

Preheat the broiler (grill). Working in batches if necessary, arrange the pepper quarters, skin side up and in a single layer, on a baking sheet. Tuck the garlic cloves under and between the peppers. Broil until the peppers are blackened and blistered, 5–7 minutes. Transfer the peppers to a brown paper bag, close tightly, and let cool for 10 minutes.

Meanwhile, squeeze the garlic cloves from their papery sheaths and cut away any burned spots. Place in a blender. Peel the roasted peppers. Place the peppers in the blender. Add the oil, lemon juice, and vinegar. Purée until smooth.

Transfer the purée to a large nonreactive saucepan and season with salt, black pepper, and cayenne. Bring to a boil over high heat. Reduce the heat to medium and simmer, uncovered, stirring frequently, until hot throughout, about 5 minutes.

Ladle the hot sauce into the jars, leaving ¼ inch (6 mm) of headspace. Remove any air bubbles and adjust the headspace, if necessary. Wipe the rims clean and seal tightly with the lids.

Process the jars for 10 minutes in a boiling-water bath (for detailed instructions, including cooling and testing seals, see pages 228–229). The sealed jars can be stored in a cool, dark place for up to 1 year. If a seal has failed, store the jar in the refrigerator for up to 1 month.

4 lb (2 kg) red, orange, or yellow bell peppers (capsicums), cut into quarters and seeded

8 cloves garlic, unpeeled

½ cup (4 fl oz/125 ml) extra-virgin olive oil

3 Tbsp fresh lemon juice

3 Tbsp balsamic vinegar

Salt and freshly ground black pepper

Cayenne pepper

Makes 5 half-pint (8–fl oz/250-ml) jars

Peaches lend mellow sweetness and a syrupy consistency to barbecue sauce. This robust sauce is best used with ribs (see page 204), chicken, or pork. It is prone to burning, so wait until the last 15 minutes of cooking before generously basting the meat.

Peach Barbecue Sauce

Have ready hot, clean jars and their lids (see page 228).

Blanch and peel the peaches (see page 234), then halve and pit. Slice the peach halves. Pour the lemon juice into a large nonreactive bowl. Add the peaches and toss to coat with the lemon juice.

In a large nonreactive saucepan over medium-low heat, warm the oil. Add the onion and cook, stirring occasionally, until tender, about 10 minutes. Add the garlic and cook for 1 minute. Stir in the peaches, sugar, vinegar, and bourbon. Bring to a boil over high heat, reduce the heat to medium, and simmer, uncovered, stirring occasionally, until the peaches and onion are very tender, about 30 minutes. Let cool.

Working in batches, transfer the peach mixture to a blender and purée until smooth. Pour into a clean, large nonreactive saucepan. Add the Worcestershire sauce, tomato paste, ginger, and chili powder. Bring to a boil over medium-high heat, reduce the heat to medium-low, and simmer, uncovered, stirring often, until hot, about 10 minutes. Season with salt and pepper.

Ladle the hot sauce into the jars, leaving ¼ inch (6 mm) of headspace. Remove any air bubbles and adjust the headspace, if necessary. Wipe the rims clean and seal tightly with the lids.

Process the jars for 15 minutes in a boiling-water bath (for detailed instructions, including cooling and testing seals, see pages 228–229). The sealed jars can be stored in a cool, dark place for up to 1 year. If a seal has failed, store the jar in the refrigerator for up to 2 weeks.

4 lb (2 kg) peaches

¼ cup (2 fl oz/60 ml) fresh lemon juice

½ cup (4 fl oz/125 ml) canola oil

1 large sweet onion such as Vidalia or Rio Sweet, coarsely chopped (about 2 cups/8 oz/250 g)

6 cloves garlic, chopped

1½ cups (10½ oz/330 g) firmly packed dark brown sugar

1 cup (8 fl oz/250 ml) cider vinegar

½ cup (4 fl oz/125 ml) bourbon or water

1 cup (8 fl oz/250 ml) Worcestershire sauce

¼ cup (2 oz/60 g) tomato paste

2 Tbsp peeled and grated fresh ginger

2 Tbsp chili powder

Salt and freshly ground pepper

Makes 4 one-pint (16–fl oz/500-ml) jars

The fruity barbecue sauce, brushed on before grilling, traps moisture and creates a luscious caramelized glaze. For a smoky flavor, partially cover the grill during cooking. Watch the ribs closely, turning to brown them evenly and removing them as soon as they are ready.

Grilled Pork Ribs with Peach Barbecue Sauce

Preheat the oven to 350°F (180°C).

Arrange the spareribs in a single layer on a baking sheet. Season on all sides with salt and pepper. Cover with aluminum foil and bake until tender, 1¼–1½ hours.

Meanwhile, prepare a charcoal or gas grill for direct grilling over medium heat, and oil the grill rack.

Remove the ribs from the oven and discard the foil. Place the ribs on the grill and brush with half of the barbecue sauce. Partially cover the grill and cook the ribs for 5–10 minutes. Turn the ribs and baste them with additional sauce. Re-cover the grill partially and continue to cook until the ribs are golden brown, 5–10 minutes longer.

Transfer the ribs to a cutting board and cut between the ribs into individual pieces. Serve at once.

6 lb (3 kg) pork spareribs, in 2 racks

Salt and freshly ground pepper

2 cups (16 fl oz/500 ml) Peach Barbecue Sauce (page 203)

Serves 6

The vibrant hue of this sweet-spicy condiment comes from the peels left on the plums during the first stage of cooking. For a lighter-colored sauce, substitute ripe green plums. Serve as an accompaniment to crisp-skinned Chinese duck, roast pork loin, or Asian-style spareribs.

Chinese-Style Plum Sauce

Have ready hot, sterilized jars and their lids (see page 228).

Halve and pit each plum, and cut each half in half. Blanch and peel the peaches (see page 234), then halve and pit. Slice the peach halves.

In a large nonreactive saucepan over medium-low heat, warm the oil. Add the onion and sauté until soft, about 5 minutes. Add the garlic, chiles, bell pepper, ginger, and ½ cup (4 fl oz/125 ml) of the vinegar. Stir in the plums and peaches. Add 1 cup (8 fl oz/250 ml) water and bring to a boil over high heat. Reduce the heat to medium-low and cook, uncovered, stirring occasionally, until the onion and fruit are tender, about 25 minutes.

Pass the plum mixture through a food mill or coarse-mesh sieve set over a bowl. Transfer to a large nonreactive saucepan. Stir in both sugars, the remaining 1 cup vinegar, five-spice powder, and salt. Bring to a boil, reduce the heat to a simmer, and cook, uncovered, stirring often, until thick, 20–30 minutes. Stir in the lemon juice.

Ladle the hot sauce into the jars, leaving ¼ inch (6 mm) of headspace. Remove any air bubbles and adjust the headspace, if necessary. Wipe the rims clean and seal tightly with the lids.

Process the jars for 10 minutes in a boiling-water bath (for detailed instructions, including cooling and testing seals, see pages 228–229). The sealed jars can be stored in a cool, dark place for up to 1 year. If a seal has failed, store the jar in the refrigerator for up to 1 month.

4 lb (2 kg) plums

2 lb (1 kg) peaches

1 Tbsp canola oil

1 large yellow onion, coarsely chopped

2 cloves garlic, minced

2 small chiles such as serrano, seeded, if desired, and finely chopped

½ jarred roasted red bell pepper (capsicum)

1 Tbsp peeled and grated fresh ginger

1½ cups (12 fl oz/375 ml) rice vinegar

2 cups (1 lb/500 g) granulated sugar

1 cup (7 oz/220 g) firmly packed light brown sugar

1 Tbsp Chinese five-spice powder, or to taste

1 Tbsp salt

1 Tbsp fresh lemon juice

Makes 5 half-pint (8–fl oz/250-ml) jars

Flavored Honey

A jar of honey, the product of an age–old dance between bees and flowers, is truly a gift of nature. You can further enhance the flavor of honey with fresh herbs, flowers, spices, and citrus.

Ingredients to Try

All sorts of flavors, from floral to piquant, complement honey's earthy sweetness. Try fresh herbs such as lavender, mint, rosemary, thyme, or lemon verbena; organic rose petals; grated citrus zest; peeled and chopped fresh ginger; spices like cinnamon, cloves, allspice, star anise, or cardamom; or add heat with red pepper flakes or a sliced fresh chile.

How to Make

Rinse and dry your flavoring ingredients (see ideas to right). Combine the honey and flavorings in the top pan of a double boiler or in a heatproof bowl. Set over (not touching) simmering water and clip a candy thermometer onto the side of the pan. Cook, stirring occasionally, until the honey reaches 185°F (85°C) on the thermometer. Simmer at 185°F for 10 minutes, stirring occasionally to prevent the honey from scorching. Remove from the heat and let stand for at least 10 minutes or up to 2 hours. Have ready a hot, sterilized jar and its lid (see page 228). For added flavor, place fresh flavoring ingredients in the jar before adding the honey. Reheat the honey over low heat until warm and strain into the jar. Seal the jar tightly. Store at room temperature for up to 1 year.

Ways to Use

Top wedges of a sheep's milk cheese such as Manchego with a drizzle of lavender-flavored honey; add apple slices or figs and Marcona almonds to round out the cheese plate. Make an Asian-inspired salad dressing with ginger-flavored honey, lime juice, rice vinegar, soy sauce, and Asian sesame oil. Stir lemon-flavored honey into a cup of hot water, and add a splash of brandy and a squeeze of lemon juice for a hot toddy.

Ginger-cardamom

For 1 cup (12 oz/375 g) honey, add 1 Tbsp fresh ginger, peeled and chopped, and 6 cardamom pods, lightly crushed.

Lavender

For 1 cup (12 oz/375 g) honey, add 6–8 fresh organic lavender sprigs or 1 Tbsp dried lavender flowers. For added flavor, place a few small lavender sprigs in the jar.

Lemon verbena

For 1 cup (12 oz/375 g) honey, add 18–20 fresh lemon verbena leaves and 1 Tbsp grated lemon zest. For added flavor, place a few lemon zest strips and a few small lemon verbena leaves in the jar.

Rose–lemon thyme

For 1 cup (12 oz/375 g) honey, add 20–25 fresh organic rose petals and 6–8 fresh lemon thyme sprigs. For added flavor, place a handful of rose petals and a few lemon thyme sprigs in the jar.

Applesauce owes its longstanding popularity to its wonderful flavor and ease of preparation. It is delicious when lightly sweetened and enlivened with lemon juice. Also try it spiked with cinnamon for breakfast or studded with fresh sage for serving alongside pork chops or sausages.

Applesauce

Have ready hot, clean jars and their lids (see page 228).

Pour the lemon juice into a large nonreactive saucepan. Core each apple and cut into chunks. As each is cut, drop the chunks into the pan and stir to coat with the lemon juice. Stir in the sugar.

Add just enough water to cover the bottom of the pan to prevent sticking. Cover and bring to a boil over high heat. Reduce the heat to medium-low and simmer, covered, stirring occasionally, until the apples are tender, about 20 minutes. Uncover and cook for 5 minutes longer.

Working in batches, pass the apple mixture through a food mill or coarse-mesh sieve set over a large bowl. Transfer to a clean saucepan. Bring to a boil over high heat, reduce the heat to medium-low, and cook, stirring, until hot. The sauce will thicken slightly during processing; ladle it into jars when it has a slightly thinner consistency than you like.

Ladle the hot applesauce into the jars, leaving ¼ inch (6 mm) of headspace. Remove any air bubbles and adjust the headspace, if necessary. Wipe the rims clean and seal tightly with the lids.

Process the jars for 20 minutes in a boiling-water bath (for detailed instructions, including cooling and testing seals, see pages 228–229). The sealed jars can be stored in a cool, dark place for up to 1 year. If a seal has failed, store the jar in the refrigerator for up to 2 weeks.

6 Tbsp (3 fl oz/80 ml) fresh lemon juice

6 lb (3 kg) apples such as Braeburn, MacIntosh, or Pink Lady

⅓ cup (3 oz/90 g) sugar

Makes 3 one-pint (16–fl oz/500-ml) jars

Cinnamon Applesauce
Stir 1 Tbsp ground cinnamon into the apple mixture after it is puréed.

Sage Applesauce
Stir 1 Tbsp minced fresh sage into the apple mixture after it is puréed.

Applesauce gives this cake a moist texture, and the icing drizzled on top adds a touch of elegance. Sprinkle chopped, toasted walnuts over the icing before it sets, and serve the cake with ice cream or whipped cream. The cake will keep for up to 3 days at room temperature.

Spiced Applesauce Cake

Preheat the oven to 350°F (180°C). Butter a nonstick Bundt pan 10 inches (25 cm) in diameter and 3 inches (7.5 cm) deep.

In a bowl, sift together the flour, cinnamon, baking soda, allspice, and salt. In another bowl, using an electric mixer on medium speed, beat the 1 cup butter and 1⅔ cups brown sugar until well blended. Add the eggs, one at a time, beating well after each addition. Beat in the vanilla. Whisk the flour mixture into the butter mixture in three batches alternately with the applesauce, whisking well after each addition. Stir in the walnuts. Pour the batter into the prepared pan.

Bake until a toothpick inserted near the center of the cake comes out clean, about 55 minutes. Transfer to a wire rack and let cool in the pan for 10 minutes. Invert the cake onto the rack and let cool.

Meanwhile, in a small saucepan over medium heat, stir together the 4 Tbsp butter and 1 Tbsp water until the butter melts. Let stand until cool, about 5 minutes. Add the ¼ cup brown sugar and stir until it dissolves. Let the butter mixture cool. Whisk in the confectioners' sugar until the icing has thickened, about 1 minute. Use the icing quickly, or it may become too thick to drizzle. If necessary, rewarm it, whisking constantly, for 2–3 minutes.

Transfer the cake to a plate and drizzle the icing evenly over the top, allowing it to run over the sides slightly. Let stand until the icing sets, about 1 hour. Cut into wedges to serve.

3⅓ cups (13½ oz/425 g) cake (soft-wheat) flour

1 Tbsp ground cinnamon

1½ tsp baking soda (bicarbonate of soda)

1 tsp ground allspice

¼ tsp salt

1 cup (8 oz/250 g) unsalted butter, at room temperature, plus 4 Tbsp (2 oz/60 g)

1⅔ cups (12 oz/375 g) firmly packed dark brown sugar, plus ¼ cup (2 oz/60 g)

3 eggs

2 tsp pure vanilla extract

2 cups (18 oz/560 g) Applesauce (facing page)

1 cup (4 oz/125 g) walnuts, toasted and chopped

½ cup (2 oz/60 g) confectioners' (icing) sugar

Makes one 10-inch (25-cm) cake

Here, a simple dry rub seasons the meat with extra flavor, and applesauce makes an ideal condiment. For a twist on the garnish, fry the sage leaves in hot oil until crisp, about 30 seconds. Sage Applesauce (see variation, page 208) would be delicious here as well.

Roasted Pork Chops with Applesauce

In a small bowl, combine the black pepper, cayenne pepper, and mustard. Add 1 Tbsp of the oil and stir to mix well. Rub the chops on both sides with the spice mix. If desired, place the chops on a plate, cover, and refrigerate for up to 1 day (remove the chops from the refrigerator about 30 minutes before roasting).

Preheat the oven to 400°F (200°C).

In an ovenproof frying pan over high heat, warm the remaining 2 Tbsp olive oil. Add the chops and sear, turning once, until golden brown on both sides, 2–3 minutes on each side. Transfer the pan to the oven. Roast the chops until the juices they release when pierced with a knife are rosy, or an instant-read thermometer inserted into the center of a chop away from the bone registers 145°–150°F (63°–65°C), 15–20 minutes.

Meanwhile, in a saucepan over low heat, warm the applesauce. Transfer the chops to a warmed platter or individual plates and garnish with the sage leaves. Pass the warmed applesauce at the table.

1 Tbsp freshly ground black pepper

Pinch of cayenne pepper

1 tsp Dijon mustard (page 194 or purchased)

3 Tbsp olive oil

4 bone-in pork loin chops, each about 10 oz (315 g) and 1½ inches (4 cm) thick

Applesauce (page 208) for serving

Fresh sage leaves for garnish

Serves 4

This fruity vinegar will breathe new life into salad dressings and sauces. It's also a wonderful gift, especially in a pretty glass bottle accompanied by a few serving suggestions. You can substitute the same amount of blueberries or raspberries for an equally tasty result.

Blackberry Vinegar

Have ready a clean, large nonreactive bowl.

Thoroughly rinse the mint leaves, if using, and then pat dry with a paper towel. Roughly chop the leaves. In a large nonreactive saucepan over low heat, warm the vinegar until hot but not yet simmering; do not let it boil. Remove from the heat. Place the blackberries and the mint, if using, in the bowl. Pour in the hot vinegar and stir to combine. Set aside to cool. Cover the bowl with plastic wrap and refrigerate for 2–4 weeks; the longer the vinegar stands, the stronger the flavor will be. Gently stir the vinegar every few days to blend the flavors.

Have ready hot, sterilized bottles (see page 228).

Strain the vinegar through a fine-mesh sieve and then through a coffee filter. Using a funnel, pour the filtered vinegar into the bottles. Cover tightly and store at room temperature for up to 2 months.

½ cup (½ oz/15 g) fresh mint leaves (optional)

4 cups (32 fl oz/1 l) white wine vinegar or rice vinegar

3 cups (12 oz/375 g) blackberries, crushed

Makes 2 one-pint (16–fl oz/500-ml) bottles

Drizzle this herb-infused vinegar over a salad of fresh tomatoes and mozzarella, or use it as a dipping sauce. Other herbs, such as rosemary, thyme, or tarragon, can be used in place of the basil. Look for long-necked glass vinegar bottles with tight-fitting corks or screw caps.

Garlic-Basil Vinegar

Have ready a clean, large nonreactive bowl.

Thoroughly rinse the basil leaves and then pat dry with paper towels. Roughly chop the leaves. In a nonreactive saucepan over low heat, warm the vinegar until hot but not yet simmering; do not let it boil. Remove from the heat. Place the basil, garlic, and lemon zest, if using, in the bowl. Pour in the hot vinegar and stir to combine. Set aside to cool. Cover the bowl tightly with plastic wrap and refrigerate for 2–4 weeks; the longer the vinegar stands, the stronger the flavor will be. Gently stir the vinegar every few days to blend the flavors.

Have ready hot, sterilized bottles (see page 228).

Strain the vinegar through a fine-mesh sieve and then through a coffee filter. Using a funnel, pour the filtered vinegar into the bottles. Cover tightly and store at room temperature for up to 2 months.

1½ cups (1½ oz/45 g) fresh basil leaves

4 cups (32 fl oz/1 l) white wine vinegar or Champagne vinegar

1 clove garlic, thinly sliced

2 lemon zest strips, each 1 inch (2.5 cm) wide and 2 inches (5 cm) long (optional)

Makes 2 one-pint (16–fl oz /500-ml) bottles

Infused Spirits

Infusing spirits with fruits, herbs, and spices is an age-old technique that is regaining popularity. You can also use spirits to preserve fruits—see page 233 for two great recipes.

Ingredients to Try

A mild-flavored alcohol like vodka is a good choice for infusing, as it doesn't overpower the infused flavors. Gin, white rum, brandy, grappa, and sake also work well. To create flavorful infusions, try using fresh herbs like lemon verbena, basil, mint, thyme, and rosemary; sliced citrus fruits; sliced apricots, peaches, and nectarines; cherries and berries; sliced cucumbers; sliced fresh ginger; fresh chiles; and rhubarb.

How to Make

Have ready a clean, widemouthed jar and its lid. Thoroughly rinse and pat dry all of the flavoring ingredients (see ideas at right). Pour the alcohol into the jar. Add the ingredients and gently push down to submerge. Wipe the rim clean and seal tightly with the lid. Store the jar in a cool, dark place, shaking it every day. After 1 week, sample the alcohol. If it has not reached the desired flavor, shake and taste it every day or two until you are satisfied with the flavor. Strain the alcohol through a fine-mesh sieve or paper coffee filter. Discard the flavorings. Return the strained alcohol to the jar and seal tightly with the lid. Store in the refrigerator for up to 2 months.

Ways to Use

Infused spirits add fresh flavor to any drink. Pour apricot-thyme gin or rhubarb vodka over ice and add a splash of soda water; garnish with a lemon wedge. Make a kumquat mojito by muddling fresh mint leaves, then adding kumquat-mint rum, soda water, and simple syrup. Make a basil gimlet by shaking basil-lime vodka, lime juice, and simple syrup in a cocktail shaker; strain into a martini glass and garnish with a basil leaf.

Apricot-thyme gin
Combine 2 cups
(16 fl oz/500 ml) gin
with 3 apricots, halved
or quartered, and
3 fresh thyme sprigs.

Basil-lime vodka
Combine 2 cups
(16 fl oz/500 ml)
vodka with 4 fresh
basil sprigs and 1 lime,
thinly sliced.

Cherry brandy
Combine 2 cups
(16 fl oz/500 ml)
brandy with 1 cup
(5 oz/155 g) cherries,
lightly crushed.

Kumquat-mint rum
Combine 2 cups
(16 fl oz/500 ml)
white rum with 10
kumquats, halved,
and 3 fresh mint sprigs.

Lemon verbena gin
Combine 2 cups
(16 fl oz/500 ml) gin
with 1 long fresh lemon
verbena sprig and
1 lemon, thinly sliced.

Rhubarb vodka
Combine 2 cups
(16 fl oz/500 ml)
vodka with 2 rhubarb
stalks, lightly crushed.

Combine good-quality extra-virgin olive oil with fresh herbs, spices, and citrus of your choice to create a delicious infusion. Toss flavored olive oils with a green salad, drizzle on tomatoes or grilled vegetables, or use as a dipping sauce for crusty bread.

Chile-Lemon Olive Oil

Have ready a hot, sterilized bottle (see page 228).

Pour the olive oil into a small nonreactive saucepan. Working directly over the pan, grate the zest from the lemons, letting it fall into the oil. Add the chiles and bay leaf. Clip a candy thermometer onto the side of the pan. Heat the oil over medium-low heat until the thermometer registers 200°F (95°C). Cook at 200°–225°F (95°–110°C) for 10 minutes. Let cool slightly.

Using a funnel, pour the oil into the bottle. Cover tightly and store at room temperature for up to 2 months.

2 cups (16 fl oz/500 ml) extra-virgin olive oil

2 large lemons

3 or 4 dried whole chiles

1 bay leaf

Makes 1 one-pint (16–fl oz/500-ml) bottle

Orange-Rosemary Oil
Substitute the zest from 1 orange for the lemon zest and 3 sprigs fresh rosemary, rinsed and patted dry, for the chiles.

This popular Italian flatbread is made in many regions of the country and prepared with different toppings, from grapes to tomato to walnuts and anchovies. Serve this simple version, topped with sea salt and herbs, with a flavored oil and vinegar dipping sauce.

Focaccia with Chile-Lemon Dipping Sauce

In a small bowl, sprinkle the yeast over the warm water and let stand until creamy, about 5 minutes. Stir until dissolved. Add the milk and 4 Tbsp (2 fl oz/60 ml) of the olive oil and stir to combine.

In a large bowl, using a wooden spoon, stir together the flour, 2 tsp salt, thyme, rosemary, and sage. Add the yeast mixture and stir until a soft dough forms, about 2 minutes. Turn out the dough onto a lightly floured work surface and knead until smooth and elastic, about 10 minutes. Shape the dough into a ball.

Oil a large bowl, place the dough in the bowl, and turn it once to coat the top. Cover the bowl with plastic wrap and let the dough rise in a warm, draft-free place until doubled in bulk, about 1 hour.

Oil a 15-by-10-inch (38-by-25-cm) baking sheet. Punch down the dough, transfer to the prepared pan, and flatten it out with your hands to cover the bottom completely. Cover with plastic wrap and let rise again in a warm place until doubled in bulk, about 1 hour.

Preheat the oven to 450°F (230°C). Using your fingertips, press down firmly into the dough to make dimples about 1 inch (2.5 cm) apart and 1 inch deep. Drizzle the entire surface with the remaining 2 Tbsp olive oil and sprinkle with coarse salt.

Bake until the focaccia is golden brown, 25–30 minutes. Slide onto a wire rack to cool completely. Pour the chile-lemon oil into a small, shallow bowl, then drizzle the balsamic vinegar on top. Cut the focaccia into squares and serve at once with the dipping sauce.

2½ tsp (1 package) active dry yeast

½ cup (4 fl oz/125 ml) warm water (105°–115°F/ 40°–46°C)

1½ cups (12 fl oz/375 ml) milk

6 Tbsp (3 fl oz/90 ml) olive oil

5 cups (1½ lb/750 g) all-purpose (plain) flour

2 tsp salt

1 tsp *each* chopped fresh thyme, rosemary, and sage, or ¼ tsp *each* dried thyme, rosemary, and sage

Coarse sea salt

⅓ cup (3 fl oz/80 ml) Chile-Lemon Olive Oil (page 216)

2 Tbsp aged balsamic vinegar

Makes one 15-by-10-inch (38-by-25-cm) focaccia

This pantry staple is easy to prepare. You don't need to peel the tomatoes, because a food mill or sieve removes the peels and most of the seeds after the tomatoes are cooked. Adding lemon juice just before processing the sauce contributes some acidity, making it safer for storage.

Tomato-Basil Sauce

Have ready hot, clean jars and their lids (see page 228).

In a large nonreactive saucepan over medium heat, warm the oil. Add the onions and cook, stirring occasionally, until translucent, 5–7 minutes. Add the garlic and cook, stirring, for 2 minutes longer.

Add the tomatoes and the wine, if using. Raise the heat to high and bring to a boil. Reduce the heat to medium and simmer, uncovered, stirring occasionally, until reduced by half, about 1 hour.

Pass the tomato mixture through a food mill or coarse-mesh sieve set over a clean, large nonreactive saucepan. Bring to a boil over medium-high heat. Reduce the heat to medium-low and simmer until the sauce reaches the desired consistency. Stir in the basil, lemon juice, salt, and pepper. Taste the sauce and adjust the seasonings.

Ladle the hot sauce into the jars, leaving ¼ inch (6 mm) of headspace. Remove any air bubbles and adjust the headspace, if necessary. Wipe the rims clean and seal tightly with the lids.

Process the jars for 30 minutes in a boiling-water bath (for detailed instructions, including cooling and testing seals, see pages 228–229). The sealed jars can be stored in a cool, dark place for up to 1 year. If a seal has failed, store the jar in the refrigerator for up to 2 weeks.

1 Tbsp olive oil

4 yellow onions, coarsely chopped

6 cloves garlic, chopped

10 lb (5 kg) tomatoes, cut into chunks

½ cup (4 fl oz/125 ml) dry red wine (optional)

½ cup (¾ oz/20 g) finely chopped fresh basil

¼ cup (2 fl oz/60 ml) fresh lemon juice

1½ tsp salt

¼ tsp freshly ground pepper

Makes 6 one-pint (16–fl oz/500-ml) jars

Appreciated for its flavorful simplicity, this traditional dish marries pasta with garden-fresh tomatoes and basil. Adding pancetta and curls of Parmesan cheese make it a more robust meal. Pair with a green salad, crusty bread, and a Chianti or Sangiovese wine.

Spaghettini with Tomato-Basil Sauce

In a large saucepan over medium heat, warm the olive oil. Add the pancetta and cook, stirring frequently, until golden, about 10 minutes. Add the onion and sauté until tender and golden, about 5 minutes. Add the garlic and chile and sauté until the garlic is golden, about 1 minute longer. Stir in the tomato sauce and keep warm over low heat.

Meanwhile, bring a large pot of water to a boil over high heat. Add the salt and pasta and cook, stirring frequently, until the pasta is al dente, according to the package directions. Drain the pasta, reserving a ladeful of the cooking water.

Add the pasta to the saucepan and stir and toss well. Add a little of the reserved cooking water to loosen the sauce, if necessary. Sprinkle with the ⅓ cup grated cheese and toss again.

Divide among warmed individual plates. Garnish with the basil and Parmesan shavings and serve at once.

2 Tbsp olive oil

¼ lb (125 g) pancetta, chopped

1 small yellow onion, chopped

1 clove garlic, chopped

1 small dried red chile, crushed, or pinch of red pepper flakes

2½ cups (20 fl oz/625 ml) Tomato-Basil Sauce (page 219)

2 tsp salt

1 lb (500 g) spaghettini or other strand pasta

⅓ cup (1½ oz/45 g) freshly grated Parmesan cheese, plus shavings for garnish

¼ cup (⅓ oz/10 g) chopped fresh basil

Serves 4–6

This syrup is the perfect partner for crêpes or slices of almond tea cake or plain pound cake. You can leave the blueberries in for a more rustic whole fruit syrup. If straining the syrup, use a coarse sieve, rather than a fine-mesh one, for a slightly thicker result.

Blueberry Syrup

Have ready hot, sterilized jars and their lids (see page 228).

In a nonreactive saucepan, stir together the blueberries, sugar, and lemon zest, if using. Add ¾ cup (6 fl oz/180 ml) water and bring to a boil over high heat. Reduce the heat to medium-low and simmer uncovered, stirring occasionally, until the blueberries are plump and some have burst, about 10 minutes.

Transfer the blueberry mixture to a fine-mesh sieve set over a bowl and press on the solids with a wooden spoon to extract as much liquid as possible. For an even finer consistency, line the sieve with cheesecloth (muslin). Return to the saucepan. Bring to a boil over high heat. Reduce the heat to medium-low and simmer, stirring, until a light, syrupy consistency, 2–5 minutes. The sauce will thicken slightly during processing; stop cooking when it has a slightly thinner consistency than you might like. Stir in the lemon juice.

Ladle the hot syrup into the jars, leaving ¼ inch (6 mm) of headspace. Remove any air bubbles and adjust the headspace, if necessary. Wipe the rims clean and seal tightly with the lids.

Process the jars for 10 minutes in a boiling-water bath (for detailed instructions, including cooling and testing seals, see pages 228–229). The sealed jars can be stored in a cool, dark place for up to 1 year. If a seal has failed, store the jar in the refrigerator for up to 1 month.

6 cups (1½ lb/750 g) blueberries

1½ cups (12 oz/375 g) sugar

1 tsp finely chopped lemon zest (optional)

3 Tbsp fresh lemon juice

Makes 3 half-pint (8–fl oz/250-ml) jars

Lavender-Blueberry Syrup
Add 3 Tbsp dried or ⅓ cup (¾ oz/20 g) fresh pesticide-free lavender flowers to the blueberries, sugar, and water.

Orange-Blueberry Syrup
Substitute the same amount of finely chopped orange zest and fresh orange juice for the lemon zest and juice.

This fruit–laden syrup doesn't take much more than 15 minutes to cook, making it one of the quickest ways to transform simple pancakes or waffles into something memorable. An inexpensive handheld cherry pitter will make short work of the pitting process.

Bing Cherry Syrup

Have ready hot, sterilized jars and their lids (see page 228).

In a large nonreactive saucepan, combine both sugars. Add 4 cups (32 fl oz/1 l) water and bring to a boil over high heat, stirring to dissolve the sugar. Continue to cook, uncovered, for 5 minutes. Add the cherries, reduce the heat to low, and simmer uncovered until the cherries are soft, 8–10 minutes. Stir in the almond extract and simmer for about 2 minutes longer to blend the flavors.

Ladle the hot syrup into the jars, leaving ¼ inch (6 mm) of headspace. Remove any air bubbles and adjust the headspace, if necessary. Wipe the rims clean and seal tightly with the lids.

Process the jars for 10 minutes in a boiling-water bath (for detailed instructions, including cooling and testing seals, see pages 228–229). The sealed jars can be stored in a cool, dark place for up to 1 year. If a seal has failed, store the jar in the refrigerator for up to 1 month.

2 cups (14 oz/440 g) firmly packed light brown sugar

2 cups (1 lb/500 g) granulated sugar

1½ lb (750 g) large Bing cherries, pitted

1 Tbsp almond extract

Makes 6 half-pint (8–fl oz/250-ml) jars

Buttermilk makes these pancakes light and fluffy. Add fresh or frozen blueberries to the batter for double-berry flavor, or use them as a garnish for the pancakes. Bing Cherry Syrup (page 223) would also be a lovely accompaniment to this classic breakfast treat.

Buttermilk Pancakes with Blueberry Syrup

Preheat the oven to 250°F (120°C). Place an ovenproof platter in the oven.

In a bowl, using an electric mixer on medium speed, beat the eggs until frothy. Add the flour, sugar, baking powder, baking soda, salt, buttermilk, and melted butter. Continue to beat just until the mixture is smooth; do not overbeat.

Heat a heavy frying pan over high heat until it is hot enough for a few drops of water to sizzle and then immediately evaporate. Brush the pan with oil. Pour about ⅓ cup (3 fl oz/80 ml) of the batter onto the hot surface. Cook until the surface is covered with tiny bubbles, the batter is set, the underside is browned, and the edges look dry, about 2 minutes. Turn the pancake and cook until the second side is golden brown, about 2 minutes longer. Transfer to the platter in the oven to keep warm. Repeat with the remaining batter, adding more oil to the pan as needed.

Serve the pancakes hot, passing the syrup at the table.

2 eggs

2 cups (10 oz/315 g) all-purpose (plain) flour

2 Tbsp sugar

2 tsp baking powder

1 tsp baking soda (bicarbonate of soda)

1 tsp salt

2 cups (16 fl oz/500 ml) buttermilk

4 Tbsp (2 oz/60 g) unsalted butter, melted

1 or 2 Tbsp canola oil

Blueberry Syrup (page 222) for serving

Makes twelve 6-inch (15-cm) pancakes; serves 4

REFERENCE

Canning Step by Step

1 Preparing the jars & lids

First, ready the jars, lids, and screw bands. Jars, whether new or previously used, should be free of chips and scratches. New lids must be used for each batch, though screw bands, if in good condition, can be reused. Wash the jars, lids, and bands well in hot soapy water, either by hand or in a dishwasher. Place the lids in a small saucepan with water to cover, bring to a simmer (180°F/82°C), and maintain the simmer until you are ready to use them. Avoid boiling the lids, or you may compromise the seal.

If the recipe processing time is more than 10 minutes, the jars need only be washed before use, since sterilization will occur during processing. If the recipe processing time is 10 minutes or less, however, the jars must be sterilized in the boiling-water canner before they are filled. To sterilize them, fill the canner pot two-thirds full of hot water. Fill the jars with hot water and, using a rubber-coated jar lifter, lower the jars, one at a time, onto the rack in the water-filled pot, making sure they are covered by at least 1 inch (2.5 cm) of water. Bring the water to a boil over high heat and boil for 10 minutes. Turn off the heat and leave the jars in the hot water. Remove them with the jar lifter and dry them as needed.

Always keep the jars warm until you are ready to fill them to ensure that they don't break when a hot mixture is added and that they seal properly. If you have cleaned the jars in a dishwasher and they don't need sterilization, leave them in the dishwasher with the door closed, removing them, one at a time, as needed. If you have sterilized them in the canner pot, leave them in the hot water until needed. You can also keep just-washed jars warm by immersing them in a large pan filled with boiling water and then turning off the heat, or by slipping them into a low oven.

2 Filling & processing the jars

If you have sterilized the jars in the water canner, the rack will already be in place. If you have not, before filling the jars, insert the rack into the canner. Fill the canner about two-thirds full with water and bring to a boil over high heat. At the same time, bring a tea kettle full of water to a boil, and then adjust the heat to maintain a simmer, in case you need additional boiling water to cover the filled jars once they are in the canner.

Working with one warm, dry jar at a time, place a funnel over the opening. Depending on the recipe, use a ladle, slotted spoon, or other utensil to fill the jars, leaving the amount of headspace called for in the recipe. To determine the headspace, measure the space between the top of the jar and the top of the food or liquid in the jar. Run a thin nonmetallic spatula or a chopstick around the inside edge of the jar to release any air bubbles trapped inside, and then adjust the headspace if necessary. Wipe the rim with a clean, damp cloth to remove any errant droplets that could prevent a proper seal. Use nonmetallic tongs or a magnetic wand to remove a hot lid from the simmering water, and dry with a clean kitchen towel. Top the jar with a dry, warm lid. Then screw a band over the lid just until it is secure. Do not turn the band too tightly, as the seal must allow air to escape from the jar during processing.

Immediately arrange the jars in the canner, using the jar lifter to lower them onto the rack. Do not let the jars cool before exposing them to boiling water, or they may crack. Make sure the jars are covered by at least 2 inches (5 cm) of water. Cover the pot with the lid and begin timing the processing after the water has returned to a rapid boil.

Once the time is up, use the lifter to remove the jars from the boiling water. Place the jars on a kitchen towel or rack, spacing them well apart to allow air to circulate, and let cool completely. You may hear the "ping" of the jar lids being sucked into a vacuum seal within minutes of removing them from the water, or it may take hours for the seal to occur.

3 Testing the seal

When the jars have cooled completely, test the seal by gently pressing on the top of each lid. It should be taut and rigid to the touch and slightly indented. If the lid bounces back and makes a clicking noise when you press it, the seal is not good. To test it further, unscrew the band and gently lift the lid with your fingertips. If you are able to pick up the entire jar by holding the edges of the lid, the seal is good. If the lid slips easily from the jar rim, the seal is insufficient. Store any jar that does not have a good seal in the refrigerator for the time specified in individual recipes.

4 Storing

Most jars with proper seals can be stored for up to 1 year. Label the jars with their contents and the date on which they were sealed, and then store in a cool, dark place, as excessive heat or light can discolor the contents. Each time you open a new jar, check the contents for signs of spoilage. Be wary if the aroma is especially sour or musty. Also, dispose of the contents of any jar with visible mold or discoloration at the top or around any air pockets, or with tiny bubbles, a sign the contents have fermented. Finally, discard the contents of any jar that does not appear to have maintained a tight seal throughout its storage.

Altitude adjustments

The recipes in this book have been formulated for canning at sea level. High altitudes require a longer processing time, because the higher the elevation, the lower the temperature at which water boils. In general, you should add 1 minute to the processing time for every 1,000 feet (300 m) in altitude, or 2 minutes per 1,000 feet if the original processing time is more than 20 minutes. For altitudes higher than 5,000 feet (1,500 m), consider using a steam-pressure canner, which will allow for accurate processing time without overcooking the food.

Kitchen tools

Because canning can be a time-sensitive process, it is important to have your ingredients prepped and any necessary kitchen tools at the ready before you begin. Along with the specialized equipment detailed on page 8, the following basic kitchen tools and supplies are helpful to have on hand:

- Blender, food processor, or food mill
- Citrus juicer or reamer
- Citrus zester
- Clean kitchen towels
- Coring and pitting utensils
- Cutting board
- Food scale
- Kitchen timer
- Sturdy ladle
- Large sieve or colander
- Long-handled spoons, slotted and unslotted
- Measuring spoons and cups
- Nonreactive mixing bowls
- Nonreactive pans
- Paring knife and chef's knife
- Pot holders, oven mitts, or heatproof gloves

About Pectin

Most fruits do not contain enough natural pectin to make jelly without added pectin. You can make your own pectin from slightly underripe apples (see recipe at right) or use store-bought. Although time-consuming to make, homemade pectin is worth the effort. You can freeze it or preserve it in jars, just as you would a jam or jelly, to have on hand for later use.

To make homemade pectin, you'll need to source small, underripe fruits. If you have access to an apple tree, select undersized, cosmetically challenged apples. At farmers' markets, apple growers may be willing to sell you large amounts of underripe fruits at a reduced price. Remember, the riper the fruit, the less pectin it will have. However, if the apples are too immature, the pectin will impart little flavor to the finished jelly. Never use apples that have been in cold storage, as they contain very little pectin.

Even with natural, homemade pectin, you will need to add a lot of sugar to your jelly. There's no way around it: forming a jell requires a proper balance of sugar, acid, and pectin. If a jelly is runny, it's because those key elements are out of balance.

If you prefer to use store-bought pectin, follow the package directions carefully to ensure that your jelly or jam sets properly. In general, 4 cups (32 fl oz/1 l) Homemade Apple Pectin is equal to about 3 fl oz (90 ml) packaged liquid pectin.

Testing homemade pectin

If you're using homemade pectin for making jelly, it's a good idea to test the strength of the pectin. Boil together the pectin, fruit juice, and acid as directed in the recipe. Before adding the sugar, remove the mixture from the heat and let cool slightly. Place about 3 Tbsp rubbing alcohol in a water glass

Pectin levels of fruit

Low	Figs, Pears, Raspberries, Rhubarb, Strawberries
Medium	Apricots, Blackberries, Blueberries, Cherries, Grapes, Nectarines, Oranges (navel), Peaches
High	Apples, Cranberries, Grapefruits, Kiwis, Lemons, Limes, Plums, Quinces

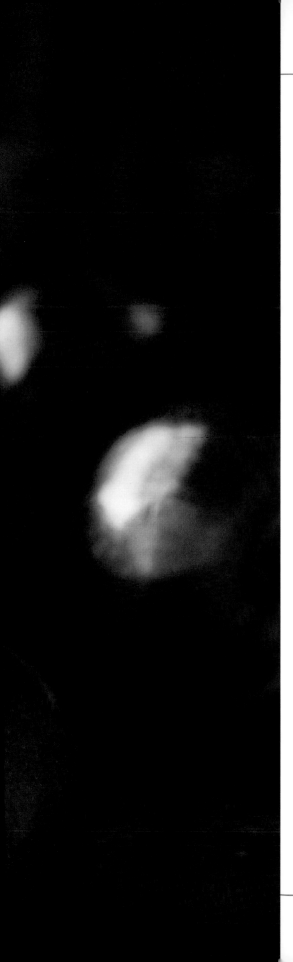

and drop about 1 tsp of the cooled pectin-juice mixture into it. If it coagulates into a single clot, the pectin is ready. If it cannot be picked up in one mass with a fork, the mixture needs to reduce more. Continue to cook for 2 or 3 minutes longer, remove from the heat, let cool slightly, and test again.

Once the pectin is ready, measure it and add an equal amount of sugar. Cook for 1 or 2 minutes more and then conduct the spoon jell test: Dip a large metal spoon in the jelly and turn it sideways over the pot. If the jelly drips in a sheet off the back of the spoon, or falls off in large drops, then it is likely ready. Before transferring the jelly to jars, conduct the plate test (below) to be sure it has set.

Testing for the jell point

Fruit spreads such as jams, jellies, and marmalades must be tested during cooking to ensure that they will jell properly once cooled. To do this, first place 2 or 3 small plates in the freezer. Cook the fruit mixture as directed in each recipe, then remove from the heat. Put 1 tsp of the mixture on a chilled plate and return to the freezer for 2 minutes. The mixture is ready if it wrinkles when nudged gently with a finger. If it doesn't, continue to cook for 1 or 2 minutes longer, remove from the heat, and test again on a clean chilled plate.

Homemade Apple Pectin

8 lb (4 kg) underripe apples such as Granny Smith or Pink Lady, stems removed

Cut the apples lengthwise into slices about ½ inch (12 mm) thick, retaining the seeds and cores. Place the apple slices in a pot and add 4 qt (4 l) water. Bring to a boil over medium-high heat and cook, stirring occasionally to prevent scorching, for 20 minutes. Remove from heat and let stand for 15 minutes.

Suspend a jelly bag over a deep nonreactive bowl and pour the apple mixture into the bag. Let the bag stand overnight. Do not squeeze the bag, or the pectin will be cloudy. The pectin should be slightly thick and slimy to the touch.

Transfer the pectin to airtight containers and refrigerate for up to 2 days or freeze for up to 2 months.

To keep the pectin for a longer period of time, warm it over medium heat, then ladle it into 4 hot, sterilized 1-pint (16–fl oz/500-ml) jars and process and store as directed for Mint Jelly (page 53).

Makes 8 cups (64 fl oz/2 l)

Additional Recipes

Blueberry Pie Filling

12 cups (3 lb/1.5 kg) blueberries

2½ cups (1¼ lb/625 g) sugar

¾ cup (3 oz/90 g) ClearJel starch

¼ cup (2 fl oz/60 ml) bottled lemon juice

Have ready hot, clean jars and their lids (see page 228).

Bring a pot of water to a boil. Add the blueberries to the boiling water and blanch for 1 minute. Drain the berries, return to the pot, and cover to keep warm.

In a large nonreactive saucepan, combine the sugar and ClearJel starch. Add 3½ cups (28 fl oz/ 875 ml) water and stir to combine. Bring to a boil over medium-high heat, stirring occasionally. Reduce the heat to medium-low and simmer, stirring constantly, until translucent and slightly thickened, 1–2 minutes. Stir in the lemon juice. Fold in the blueberries and stir until warm, if necessary.

Ladle the hot blueberry mixture into the jars, leaving 1 inch (2.5 cm) of headspace. Remove any air bubbles and adjust the headspace, if necessary. Wipe the rims clean and seal tightly with the lids.

Process the jars for 30 minutes in a boiling-water bath (see pages 228–229). The sealed jars can be stored in a cool, dark place for up to 1 year. If a seal has failed, store the jar in the refrigerator for up to 1 week.

Makes 7 one-pint (16–fl oz/500-ml) jars

Basic Pie Pastry

For a single-crust pie

1½ cups (7½ oz/235 g) all-purpose (plain) flour

½ tsp salt

½ cup (4 oz/125 g) vegetable shortening

3–4 Tbsp cold water

For a double-crust pie

2¼ cups (111/2 oz/360 g) all-purpose (plain) flour

¾ tsp salt

¾ cup (6 oz/185 g) vegetable shortening

6–7 Tbsp cold water

Combine the flour, salt, and shortening in the work bowl of a food processor. Process with 15 rapid off-on pulses; the mixture should be light and dry and resemble tiny flakes. Add 2 Tbsp water (4 Tbsp for a double-crust pie) and process in 5 rapid pulses. Add 1 more Tbsp water (2 Tbsp for a double-crust pie) and process in 3 rapid pulses. If necessary, add water by teaspoonfuls, processing for an instant after each addition, until the dough begins to come together in a mass but does not form a ball.

With floured hands, pat the dough into a smooth disk (for a double-crust pie, make 2 disks, one slightly larger than the other). Use immediately, or wrap in plastic wrap and refrigerate for up to 2 days.

Rolling out the dough and lining the pan: On a lightly floured surface, roll the dough out (using the larger piece if making a double-crust pie) into a 12-inch (30-cm) round. Transfer the rolled-out pastry to the pie pan. Pat the pastry in around the edges to fit the pan's shape.

If you are making a single-crust pie, trim the edges to form a ¾-inch (2-cm) overhang. Fold the overhang under itself and pinch to create a high edge on the rim of the pan. If you are making a double-crust pie, do not trim the edges of the bottom crust. Roll out the remaining pastry for the top crust and set it aside on waxed paper. After filling the pie shell, place the second dough round over the filling. Trim the edge of the bottom and top crust together so they are even, leaving a ¾-inch (2-cm) overhang. Fold the overhang under itself and pinch to create a high edge on the rim of the pan. Using a sharp knife, cut 3 or 4 slits in the center of the top crust to make steam vents.

Makes one 9-inch (23-cm) pie crust

Blackberries & Grappa

1 cup (8 oz/250 g) sugar

3 cups (¾ lb/375 g) blackberries
or olallieberries

½ cup (4 fl oz/125 ml) grappa
or eau-de-vie

Have ready a hot, clean jar and
its lid (see page 228).

In a small nonreactive saucepan,
combine the sugar and 1 cup
(8 fl oz/250 ml) water. Bring to
a boil over medium-high heat,
stirring to dissolve the sugar.
Reduce the heat to medium,
add the blackberries, and cook
gently, stirring occasionally, for
2 minutes.

Using a slotted spoon, transfer the
hot berries to the jar, packing them
firmly. Continue to cook the syrup
over medium heat until slightly
thickened and reduced by about
one-fourth, about 5 minutes.
Remove the syrup from the heat
and stir in the grappa.

Strain the hot syrup over the
berries, leaving ½ inch (12 mm)
of headspace. Remove any air
bubbles. Wipe the rim clean
and seal tightly with the lid.

Process the jar for 15 minutes in
a boiling-water bath (see pages
228–229). The sealed jar can be
stored in a cool, dark place for
up to 1 year. If the seal has failed,
store the jar in the refrigerator for
up to 2 weeks.

Makes 1 one-pint (16–fl oz/500-ml) jar

Brandied Apricots

1 lb (500 g) apricots, peaches,
or nectarines

1 cup (8 oz/250 g) sugar

½ cup (4 fl oz/125 ml) brandy

Have ready a hot, clean jar and
its lid (see page 228).

Blanch and peel the apricots (see
page 234), then cut them into
quarters and remove the pits.

In a small nonreactive saucepan,
combine the sugar and 1 cup (8 fl
oz/250 ml) water. Bring to a boil
over medium-high heat, stirring to
dissolve the sugar. Reduce the heat
to medium, add the apricots, and
cook gently, stirring occasionally,
for 3 minutes. Using a slotted spoon,
transfer the hot apricots to the jar,
packing them firmly. Continue to
boil the syrup over medium heat
until slightly thickened and reduced
by one-fourth, about 5 minutes.
Remove from the heat and stir in
the brandy.

Strain the liquid over the apricots,
leaving ½ inch (12 mm) of headspace.
Remove any air bubbles. Wipe
the rim clean and seal tightly
with the lid.

Process the jar for 20 minutes in
a boiling-water bath (see pages
228–229). The sealed jar can be
stored in a cool, dark place for up
to 1 year. If the seal has failed,
store the jar in the refrigerator
for up to 2 weeks.

Makes 1 one-pint (16–fl oz/500-ml) jar

Preserved Limes

8 limes

8 tsp plus 1 Tbsp kosher salt

1½ cups (24 fl oz/750 ml) fresh lime
juice, or as needed

3 jalapeño chiles, cut into slices
½ inch (12 mm) thick (optional)

Have ready a hot, sterilized jar
and its lid (see page 228).

Scrub each lime thoroughly under
cold running water to remove
any dirt or wax. Cut each lime
lengthwise into quarters, leaving
them attached at the stem end.
Gently spread apart each quarter
and sprinkle 1 tsp salt into the
center. Place 1 Tbsp salt in the jar
and pack the limes into the jar,
layering in the chile slices, if using.
Pour in enough lime juice to cover
the limes, leaving ½ inch (12 mm)
of headspace. Seal the jar tightly.

Store the limes in a cool, dark
place for 3 weeks, turning the
jar occasionally to distribute
the lime juice and salt evenly.
Preserved limes can be stored
in the refrigerator for up to
6 months.

Makes 1 one-quart (1-l) jar

Techniques & Yields

Blanching This technique is useful for loosening the skins of stone fruits (like peaches, apricots, and nectarines) and some vegetables (such as tomatoes and onions) to ease peeling. Bring a large pot of water to a boil. Have ready a bowl of ice water. Cut a small, shallow X in the bottom of each fruit. Working in batches if necessary, add the fruit to the boiling water and blanch for 30 seconds. Using a slotted spoon, transfer the fruit to the ice water. Drain the fruit and then peel off the skins, starting at the X.

Hulling strawberries Insert a paring knife at an angle into the strawberry flesh until it reaches the middle of the top part of the berry, then make a circular cut to release the hull.

Juicing citrus fruit Press and roll the citrus fruit firmly against the work surface to loosen the membranes holding the juice, then cut the fruit in half crosswise. For small amounts of juice, use a citrus reamer to pierce the membranes as you turn and squeeze the fruit. Catch the juice in a bowl and strain it to remove the seeds. For larger amounts of juice, use a citrus press or electric juicer.

Peeling & coring apples Using a vegetable peeler, starting at the stem end, remove the peel from

the flesh in a circular motion. Halve the peeled apple from stem to blossom end. Turn the halves flat side down and cut them in half again to make quarters. If desired, rub the flesh with a cut lemon to prevent browning. Using a paring knife, make an angled incision into the center on each side of the core, creating a V cut and releasing the core. Repeat with the remaining quarters. To core a whole apple using an apple corer, hold the apple upright and firmly push the corer straight down through the apple.

Peeling & coring pears Holding the pear at a slight angle and starting at the stem end, use a vegetable peeler to remove strips of peel, rotating the pear until all of the peel is gone. Halve the peeled pear lengthwise. If desired, rub the flesh with a cut lemon to prevent browning. Use a melon baler to scoop the seeds from a pear half and to create a shallow channel from the core to the stem. Repeat with the remaining half.

Pitting cherries Using a paring knife, cut around the whole cherry to cut it in half. Rotate the halves in opposite directions to separate them. Use your fingers or the knife to pry the pit from the cherry. To pit a cherry using a cherry pitter, position the cherry, stem side up,

in the cradle of the pitter. Hold the pitter over a small bowl and press down, ejecting the pit into the bowl.

Pitting stone fruits Using a paring knife, cut the fruit in half lengthwise, cutting along either side of the crease on top of the fruit and around the pit at the center. Rotate the halves in opposite directions to separate them. Use the tip of the knife to gently dig under the pit and ease it out.

Roasting apricot or peach kernels Preheat the oven to 350°F (180°C). Place the pits on a rimmed baking sheet and bake for 10–15 minutes. Remove from the oven and leave the oven on. When the pits are cool enough to handle, remove the inner kernels: Grip each pit with pliers so that the edge is visible above the pliers. Hit the edge of the pit with a hammer until the pit cracks open and the kernel can be removed intact. Place the kernels on the baking sheet and roast for 5 minutes.

Seeding chiles Many cooks wear disposable latex gloves when working with hot chiles. Using a paring knife, halve the chile lengthwise, then cut it into quarters. Cut away the seeds and ribs from each chile quarter and slice off any stem at the top. Removing the seeds and ribs will lessen the heat of the chile.

Seeding & juicing pomegranates
To seed a pomegranate, first quarter it, and then drop the quarters into a large bowl of water. Working underwater, remove the seeds, which will fall to the bottom of the bowl, then scoop off the peel and pith floating on top and drain. Rather than juice the pomegranate as you would an orange (which can impart a bitter flavor from the membrane), remove the seeds and place them in a nonreactive saucepan. Cover and cook over medium-low heat for 20–25 minutes. Press the seeds through a fine-mesh sieve to strain the juice. You will need about 6 pomegranates for 1 cup (8 fl oz/250 ml) juice.

Toasting nuts Place the nuts in a dry frying pan over medium heat and toss and stir to prevent burning. When the nuts are golden brown, after 2–3 minutes, transfer them to a plate.

Zesting citrus Try to buy organic, unwaxed citrus fruits if you plan to use the peel. To finely grate zest, use a microplane or rasp-style grater that is designed for zesting citrus. A cocktail citrus zester is perfect for removing long, thin curls of zest. A vegetable peeler or paring knife works well for removing long strips of zest. Always use the colored part of the peel, avoiding the bitter white pith.

Estimating fruit and vegetable yields

PRODUCE	QUANTITY PER LB	YIELD
Apples	3 medium	3 cups sliced per lb
Apricots	8 to 10 medium	2–3 cups sliced per lb
Asparagus	1 bunch (16 to 20 spears)	3 cups sliced per lb
Bell peppers (capsicums)	1 or 2 large	1¼ cups chopped per lb
Berries	3 to 4 cups	2 cups per pint
Cherries	3¼ cups	
Cucumbers	1 medium	2 cups sliced per lb
Cucumbers, pickling (Kirby)	10 to 14	3 cups sliced per lb
Figs	10 to 12 medium	
Lemons/juice	3 or 4 medium	2–3 Tbsp juice per lemon
Limes/juice	5 to 7 medium	1–2 Tbsp juice per lime
Onions	3 or 4 medium	2½ cups chopped per lb
Oranges/juice	2 or 3 medium	⅓ cup juice per orange
Peaches	2 or 3 medium	2¾ cups sliced per lb
Pears	3 medium	2½ cups sliced per lb
Plums	4 or 5 medium	2½ cups sliced per lb
Quinces	1 or 2 medium	
Rhubarb	6 to 8 stalks	3 cups chunks per lb
Tomatoes	3 to 5 medium	2–3 cups chopped per lb
Zucchini (courgettes)	3 or 4 medium	3 cups sliced per lb

Index

REFERENCE

REFERENCE

weldon**owen**

415 Jackson Street, Suite 200, San Francisco, CA 94111

Telephone: 415 291 0100 Fax: 415 291 8841

www.weldonowen.com

A division of

BONNIER

WELDON OWEN, INC.	**THE ART OF PRESERVING**
CEO and President Terry Newell	Conceived and produced by Weldon Owen, Inc.
Senior VP, International Sales Stuart Laurence	and Williams-Sonoma, Inc.
VP, Sales and Marketing Amy Kaneko	Copyright © 2010 Weldon Owen, Inc. in collaboration
Director of Finance Mark Perrigo	with Williams-Sonoma, Inc.
	All rights reserved, including the right of reproduction
VP and Publisher Hannah Rahill	in whole or in part in any form.
Associate Publisher Amy Marr	
Associate Editor Julia Nelson	Color separations by Embassy Graphics in Canada
Editorial Assistant Becky Duffett	Printed and Bound by Toppan Leefung Printing Limited in China
Associate Creative Director Emma Boys	First printed in 2010
Art Director Kara Church	10 9 8 7 6 5 4 3 2 1
Designer Meghan Hildebrand	
Production Director Chris Hemesath	Library of Congress Cataloging-in-Publication
Production Manager Michelle Duggan	data is available.
Color Manager Teri Bell	ISBN-13: 978-1-74089-978-9
	ISBN-10: 1-74089-978-4
Photographer France Ruffenach	
Food Stylist Lillian Kang	All photography by France Ruffenach except for the following
Prop Stylist Sara Slavin	image: Jeff Tucker & Kevin Hossler, page 230–231.

ACKNOWLEDGMENTS

Weldon Owen wishes to thank Carrie Bradley, Ken della Penta, Judith Dunham, Lesli Neilson, and Sharon Silva for their generous support in producing this book. Rick Field wishes to thank his mom and dad for showing him how to pickle; Jonathan for making pickling interesting; Lauren McGrath and Jina Kim of Rick's Picks; Kate Galassi; Steve Mark; Joanne Wilson and all the friends of Rick's Picks; Bob Mecoy; Luc Roels; Judy Savage; Lefty; and most importantly, Susie, Alice, and Madeline. Rebecca Courchesne wishes to thank everyone at Frog Hollow Farm, especially Jose and the kitchen crew, for their help and support; Amy and Julie at Weldon Owen for being infinitely patient; her mother and Gloria for helping with the girls; and Al for growing such delicious fruit and giving her the opportunity to cook with it, and Maddie and Millie, who make everything taste sweeter.